A Wheelbarrow and a Shovel

A Wheelbarrow and a Shovel
The Story Behind America's Most Unlikely Real Estate Empire

Published by Forefront Books.

Cover Design by Bruce Gore, Gore Studio Inc.
Interior Design by Bill Kersey, KerseyGraphics

ISBN: 978-1-63763-031-0 print
ISBN: 978-1-63763-032-7 e-book

JOHN BOLL

A Wheelbarrow and a Shovel

The Story Behind America's
Most Unlikely Real Estate Empire

Forefront
BOOKS

Table of Contents

Dedication

THIS BOOK IS DEDICATED TO MY WIFE, MARLENE, without whose love and unrelenting support this life story would have never been written. To my parents, thank you for taking the ultimate "trust me" chance and allowing me to realize the American dream. To my adult children and grandchildren, each one of you was a gift from the beginning and has a special place in my heart. To the many friends who made an indelible mark in my life, thank you for the memories. And to God, thank you for my life. I don't thank you enough, but I wouldn't have lived my life any other way.

> *"It is not what you gather, but what you scatter*
> *that tells what kind of life you have lived."*
> —HELEN WALTON

Introduction

FOR MY FAMILY AND FRIENDS, SOMETIMES IT might seem as if they're in the movie *Raiders of the Lost Ark*, and I'm the Harrison Ford character—close calls and all. I'm always right there with them through the adventure and urging them, "Trust me." But sometimes my fellow actors wonder if even that is enough.

George Clark has been one of my main sidekicks in such episodes. One time, George and his wife, Letitia, and another couple chartered a 78-foot sailboat with us to explore the Caribbean. We anchored the *Swept Away* off the beautiful island of St. Lucia, and I got around to enlisting George in my next goal: conquering one of the famous twin peaks of the island, Gros Peton and Petit Peton.

These two mountains are iconic features of the Caribbean landscape. Each rises directly out of the sea and is covered all around by a carpet of trees; Gros Peton rises to a height of more than 2,600 feet and Petit Peton, to a mere 2,400 feet. Yet they can be conquered by everyday people in good physical shape without benefit of pitons, ropes, or pulleys. So the Petons have been a magnetic attraction to climbers for centuries—and that's exactly how they presented themselves to me on that day.

George wasn't as attracted. "Petit Peton is a vertical cone pretty much straight up and fairly high," he said. "It has a pitch like a dunce cap." So the first thing we thought is, "How can we do that?" We found a kid, maybe thirteen years old, who said he could take us up. The resorts around there have lots of guides like that. But it was clear right away that this kid was not any more familiar with how to get up Petit Peton than we were.

Yet we climbed and kept climbing and got about 80 percent up the mountain. Suddenly huge stones started falling on us from up above—they were four to six inches in diameter. They kept coming at us, but fortunately the trees were deflecting them away from us. So we got a little higher and I saw that someone was throwing stones at us—it wasn't accidental! The goats at the top of the peak were doing it. And they weren't stopping! Either one of us could have been killed by one of the rocks that came down. I said, "I think we'd better terminate this hike and go back down," so we did.

At the same time, George said, the episode also was characteristic of me because ". . . he lived on the edge. It wasn't something you visibly saw or that was obvious to anybody. But he pushed himself, and he pushed other people. He pushed me to do things I never would have dreamed of doing."

⸺⸺⸺⸻

The byword of my life has been "trust me." As my grandson, JT Mestdagh, saw it, when Papi said, "Trust me," it was meant to convey a can-do attitude. "He's saying, 'It may be challenging, but you're going to get through it,' " JT said.

Actually, sometimes I would say, "Trust me," even when I wasn't entirely sure I could be trusted for the result. But I guess it was a sign of my character that people generally followed anyway.

I encouraged people to "trust me" as far back as many can remember, to when I was still the young son of Dutch immigrants who risked everything to realize the American dream. I'm sure that's where I got the courage and confidence to try things others wouldn't dare do.

For example, on our family's boat trip to Europe when my sister Diena and I were just eight and nine years old, respectively, I would grab her hand and imply that she should trust me as we sneaked into the first-class section from our berths in tourist class.

"He was a rascal like that from the start," Diena said. "And he never let up. His favorite words were, 'Trust me; you can do it. You can do it. Just trust me!' He was even doing that when we were both about seventy years old and he'd taken us on this cruise in the Mediterranean, and he dared me to jump off the boat into the water. Now we have pictures of us both swimming in the sea with our heads bobbing above the water."

Most people who've spent any amount of time with me intrinsically understand the "trust me" theme. They saw it play out in my relationships in business, philanthropy, and every realm of life. In everyday settings, my invitation to trust and have confidence in me was simply implied—but also tacitly reinforced by everything about my behavior.

"One thing about John is that, if he had a contract, he would do it by handshake," said Bob Starnes, a friend through Christian circles. "His word was in his trust." Another friend, Mike Timmis, said that "...other honest and trustworthy people lined up to do business with me."

Within my family, it got to be such an apparent truth that at one point, my secretary Pam Davis requested from the Colorado DMV a personalized license plate that said "TRSTME" and put it on a butterscotch-colored Mercedes-Benz that we drove to leave at Beaver Creek. This was especially appropriate given that, as an infamously too-fast driver, I was known to yell out, "Ziggy, zaggy, ziggy, zaggy" while swerving in a car and giving my children and grandchildren many white-knuckle moments.

In so many ways, the mantra "Trust Me" has been the story of my life. From my courtship of my wife, Marlene, to the early business relationships I established as a young developer, earning others' trust through honesty, hard work, and dependability became hallmarks of my career, which culminated in becoming the first businessman to take a collection of manufactured home communities to Wall Street.

A bold idea that started with only a wheelbarrow and a shovel became what others have called one of the most unlikely success stories in American business. In the pages that follow, you'll read about the incredible characters, events, and tragedies that I encountered along the way.

It's a rags-to-riches tale could only happen in America—and only with the hand of God leading the way.

It's the adventure of a lifetime, with so many twists and turns, but I'll take your hand and guide you through.

Just trust me.

CHAPTER 1

IN THE SUMMER OF 1952, I WAS A TWENTY-year-old Army corporal from Detroit, training as a medic and stationed at Fort Bragg, North Carolina. Along with four base buddies, I was enjoying the freedom of a weekend pass as we cruised town in our civvies, open to any adventure that might come our way.

I had saved enough money working in auto plants back home to buy my first automobile—a 1949 Mercury. After six months of basic training, the Army allowed me the privilege of keeping it on base. Raleigh, North Carolina, about a half-hour ride away, was one of our favorite destinations.

My Mercury was hard to miss, a powder blue beauty that I was easily maneuvering—I'd learned to drive in automotive madness of the Motor City. During that Saturday midafternoon cruise, we pulled up at a stoplight. Immediately, we couldn't help but notice who else was at the intersection.

"What are you ladies doing standing on the corner?" my buddy Pete yelled out from the front passenger window at five attractive and unusually leggy young women. The ladies looked lost. They talked hurriedly over one another, clearly upset.

That's because they were late for a rehearsal. They had missed their bus to the North Carolina State Fair, where they were performing. They were dancers from the Roxy Theater just off Times Square in New York, known as The Roxyettes, and were scheduled to perform that evening along with nineteen colleagues in a high-kicking exhibition of athleticism, coordination, and stamina. Walking several miles to the fairgrounds simply wasn't an option: If they were late for a rehearsal, Roxy docked their pay.

Obviously, catcalls from lunkheads like us were the least of their concerns. Yet something about Pete's greeting caught one girl's attention. His rough, thick Brooklyn accent was a homing beacon for Melva, who was from the very same New York City borough. Not only did it sound reassuringly familiar and out of place in the land of syrupy Southern drawls, it made her think we were probably good guys.

"Are you from Brooklyn?" Melva chirped back. "We really need a ride. We're going to be late for our rehearsal!"

Thinking through the situation quickly and being cordial as always, I came up with a solution. I ordered the other guys to "give up your seats" and get out of my car at the curb, letting the young ladies slide in as the men exited. I would get the girls to their rehearsal on time, I told my buddies. The fairgrounds were about ten minutes away—and then I would return to pick them up.

In the weeks that followed, my fellow medics-in-training would tease me about masterminding those few seconds, though I knew well that events unfolded too quickly for me to have planned anything at all. Still, I couldn't have written a better script for how the scenario played out. Marlene Miller, a strikingly beautiful young woman from New Jersey, jumped into the front seat next to me.

"I didn't look up, look at him, or look anywhere in the car," Marlene remembered. "We were in such a hurry. I just got in— and there he was."

But I watched Marlene the entire way to the fairgrounds. I couldn't take my eyes off her, as my heart skipped a beat—or three. Right then and there, I knew she was the kind of woman I wanted to spend the rest of my life with. It just took her a while to realize it too.

———

When U.S. President Franklin Delano Roosevelt died on April 12, 1945, less than three months into his fourth term, Vice President Harry S. Truman took his place in the White House. After the end of World War II, the U.S. was able to maintain its military forces with only volunteers. But when the Cold War started heating up, Truman recommended to Congress that the draft be reinstated. The Korean War draft required men between the ages of eighteen-and-a-half to thirty-five to serve an average of two years of active service. We never knew when our names would be pulled, but it was inevitable.

I was working on small-bore construction in Detroit with my father when Uncle Sam summoned me to Fort Bragg. The Korean War was just entering its third year, with armistice negotiations stalled and the action on the battlefields of the far Asian peninsula also at a stalemate. So the U.S. Army needed to keep training new recruits at Fort Bragg, the largest defense installation in the world. I was one of the thousands at the base who'd never imagined themselves being in North Carolina, much less Korea.

While the locals in Raleigh certainly appreciated the wartime contributions made to the local economy by Fort Bragg and its soldiers, they were still uneasy about many of the strangers in town. Perhaps their biggest concern was that most of us were Yankees—and less than a century removed from the Civil War, there was still plenty of local resentment against people from north of the Mason-Dixon line. Many families in Raleigh were the ancestors of slaveholding tobacco farmers, and the succeeding generations had vivid memories of the War Between the States and its horrors for their clans.

Making matters worse for us, many of the draftees from the North were chosen to fill out the 31st Infantry Division, which was commonly known as the "Dixie Division." I'm still not sure how a Yankee ended up in the Dixie Division. It was originally organized in 1917 during World War I from national guardsmen in Alabama, Florida, and Georgia, and then its men were mobilized to fight in the South Pacific during World War II.

Of course, I stood out like a sore thumb because of my Northern accent. Obviously, it was something I couldn't hide. As part of our hazing, guys from the North were made to salute the Confederate flag. After a while, it reached a point where the Army ordered all Confederate flags to be removed from Fort Bragg, except for one—the Dixie Division flag. That made the Southerners resent us even more. Eventually, because we were working and living together, we figured out how to get along.

I was among sixteen men who were selected to train to become medics. I didn't know much about medicine or first aid. Once I completed basic training, the Army sent me to Fort Sam Houston in San Antonio for medical school. Then I was deployed to Camp Stoneman in Pittsburgh, California. It was from there I would leave to fight in Korea—or so I thought.

In the early morning in which I was supposed to load a boat to be ferried to a troop ship, which would carry me nearly 5,000 nautical miles to Korea, I was suddenly pulled out of line. An Army clerk explained to me that I had been red-listed.

"Corporal, your clothing records have not followed you here from Fort Sam Houston," he told me. "We'll have no way to keep tabs on your clothing, so we need to keep you here until your clothes catch up with you."

At the time, I couldn't have known that my displaced clothes would keep me from having to go to Korea altogether. Looking back now, I can only believe that it was divine intervention. For whatever reason, God stepped in and changed the course of my life. I have to believe that He prevented me from going to Korea—just as it had been His plan for me to meet Marlene at that intersection in Raleigh.

There was another complication for all of us soldiers at Fort Bragg: Girls of Marlene's era across America, not just in the South, had been told time and time again by their elders about the dangers of mixing socially with servicemen. For whatever reason, it wasn't considered proper to date soldiers back then. Mothers and fathers preferred that their daughters socialize with doctors, lawyers, and college students. Despite the fact that an earlier generation of GIs had rescued the world for democracy and sacrificed their lives by the thousands for their country, the soldiers in training for the Korean War weren't respected in the same manner. In fact, The Roxyettes' management even forbade its dancers from dating guys in the military while they were on their East Coast tour.

Of course, my buddies and I had already figured out how to get around both forms of cultural disapproval while we were training at Fort Bragg: We simply made up a story about ourselves. We agreed that if we met any girls, we would not tell them we were in the Army. Instead, we would say we were going to college to become doctors. Over and over again, we programed ourselves to do just that. That little white lie would explain our Northern accents, and because we were training to become medics and were familiar with medical terminology, we could use it to complete the ruse. So when we'd go to Raleigh for the weekend, we would get our civvies out of my trunk, get a hotel room, and change—and then we were everyday people, except for our voices.

As fate would have it, Marlene was in Raleigh that day chasing her dream to become a professional dancer against all odds. As the youngest of six children from a blended family—and the only offspring of her biological parents—she was heavily relied upon by her mother to stay around home; her father had died two years earlier. Yet after growing up dancing as a little girl, and then training intensely during high school, Marlene very much wanted to try her dancing dreams at the next level.

Her mom reluctantly agreed to let Marlene audition at the Roxy Theater in New York, where she knew the choreographer. The theater hired Marlene as part of a chorus line show for the summer that would start in Canada and wind down the East Coast to the Carolinas. The summer gig would have the combined benefits of allowing Marlene to hone her dance skills and to further develop her professionalism, as well as help her mother pay some bills. Once Marlene finished the tour, she would return to her home in Roselle, New Jersey, to finish high school.

Blonde, beautiful, and poised, when this 18-year-old woman plunked herself down next to me in the Mercury that day, I knew right away that she was the most intriguing person I had ever met. Certainly, she was the most striking woman I'd ever seen; I couldn't take my eyes off her. And once she looked into my eyes, it only took about five or six hours for my courtship to begin in earnest.

As the girls climbed out of my car, one of them forced a pile of tickets for their show into my hand. I fully intended to use at least one for myself—even if I had to leave all the other guys twiddling their thumbs in some park for a couple of hours. After driving Marlene and her friends to the fairgrounds, I did faithfully turn around and pick up my entourage, who were still hanging out at the intersection.

Pete had taken a liking to Melva too. So that evening all of us went to see The Roxyettes. One of their routines involved dancing across a "floor" consisting of wooden balls about two feet in diameter, an impressive display of agility and nimbleness. It was quite a sight, even if I couldn't take my eyes off one particular dancer the entire time.

By the end of their show, it was quite late, but the ten of us still went out for a bite to eat. The girls asked us why we were in town—and of course, as I told you earlier, we were more than prepared for that question. We knew that admitting we were in the Army wouldn't be a smart answer, so we instead shared our story that we were all attending medical school in Columbia.

Even our choice of a fictional home was very deliberate. The capital of South Carolina, about 200 miles to the south, was close enough to make our story about weekend visits to Raleigh convincing, but it wasn't nearly close enough for anyone to be able to check out the story in person.

I did almost get tripped up by another bit of fiction. I forgot that I made the trip to Raleigh with a Band-Aid prominently displayed on my forehead, where I'd been scraped by another soldier's boot in a training exercise. When Marlene asked me about it, I scrambled for an explanation and told her I'd gotten into a college fight. She didn't think much about it, fortunately.

As the evening wrapped up, the girls announced they were moving on to Charlotte, North Carolina, for a show the next weekend and asked if we'd like to meet them there. We promised to see if we could arrange it, though in my mind I figured getting Army passes two weekends in a row for all five of us might not be in the cards.

Much to our surprise, our entire group managed to get permission to leave Fort Bragg the next weekend as well, and we faithfully showed up in Charlotte to see The Roxyettes—and take the girls out on the town again. It was at that show where I unfurled a white handkerchief and waved it at Marlene so that she spotted me in the crowd, a gesture that I would repeat whenever I attended one of her shows from then on. After a few hours together that evening, the group broke up. The girls had reached the end of their tour and were scheduled to take off for New York the next day.

While there were varying degrees of mutual romantic interest among the others, Pete and I were clearly smitten with Melva and Marlene. Pete promised to write to Melva, and I certainly planned to stay in touch with Marlene.

For me, it wasn't just that Marlene was gorgeous, intelligent, warm, and responsive to my interest. She wasn't Dutch—and she certainly hadn't been raised in the Dutch Reform church as I had. But she was a mainline Protestant, and that was about as far from my denomination as I wanted to stray—or my devout parents would have allowed me to go. I knew my parents would have concerns about Marlene's chosen profession since the Dutch Reformed frowned upon dancing.

In addition to being dazzled by her beauty and her confidence, I sensed a depth and sincerity in Marlene. When we began to open up to each other, we recognized a sort of shared background in our difficulties and challenges, as well as our hopes and dreams.

I'll be honest: I'm not sure Marlene was as captivated by me in the beginning as I was with her. I learned years later that she appreciated my confidence, my easy way with words, and my gentlemanly manner. And, of course, she liked the fact she would have a boyfriend who was going to be a doctor—or so she thought!

However, she did have serious concerns that I was going to school in South Carolina and hailed from Detroit. Because of her obligations at home, she was pretty bound to the New York City area for the foreseeable future. Marlene just didn't see any way around the geographic challenges to start a serious relationship with me.

Nonetheless, I did my best to reassure Marlene about the future I envisioned for us—even if she couldn't see it yet. As we exchanged addresses in Charlotte—hers, the real one in Roselle, and mine the address of a conspiring friend in Columbia—I looked deeply into her eyes.

"Marlene, just trust me," I told her.

CHAPTER 2
Dreamers and Builders

THE CAPTAIN OF THE SHIP KNEW EXACTLY what was on the minds of many of the passengers who'd just boarded his steamer in the Netherlands. They were bound for a new life in the United States, and for various reasons—opportunity, shame, adventure, escape, economic necessity, family bonds that had been stretched across the Atlantic Ocean—or some combination of these.

Now chugging into the North Atlantic on a midsummer journey accompanied by friendly nautical breezes, hundreds of Dutch men, women, and children harbored a variety of emotions as well as motives. Many were hopeful; many were anxious. Lots of them also were bracing for the homesickness they knew would follow them from their familiar Holland to a fresh start in America.

"In about eight days, start watching the horizon for a green statue," the captain of the ship told Anton and Alberdiena Boll that day in late June 1928, after they boarded the ship.

The newly married couple from Groningen, in the northern Netherlands, had heard for years about the Statue of Liberty in New York's harbor, and about Ellis Island where immigrants were processed. They understood that seeing the iconic, towering "Lady Liberty" would signal their imminent arrival in their new land.

Beyond that, the Bolls knew little about what they would encounter in America. Only Anton spoke a little English. There wouldn't be a translator greeting them with a beckoning sign when they got off the ship. And they certainly didn't have relatives in New York, or anywhere else in America, who would be eagerly gobbling them up with hugs and kisses, huddling around them once they disembarked from the steamer, ushering them to safety, security, and love.

No, Anton and Alberdiena Boll, who would soon thereafter become my parents, had only each other when they arrived in New York City in early July, shortly after Independence Day and under the unflinching gaze of the grand and glorious statue. So it would be up to them, and the providence of God, to figure out their future in America.

⌒

The Bolls trace their lineage in the Netherlands at least back to 1678, when a patriarch, Frederick "Frik" Everts, registered as a member at a church near Zoutkamp, a fishing village on the far northeastern fringes of Holland. But the Boll ancestry goes back much further, before these things were recorded, because even in the late 1600s the clan was recognized as one of the oldest living in the town, according to Wija Friso, a niece of my father living in the Netherlands and the dedicated family historian.

My family and its name are tied clearly to where my ancestors lived and what they did for a living. For centuries, Zoutkamp was known—and still is today—for harvesting the gray-colored shrimp that are abundant in a canal just a few miles from the North Sea. To this day, the Dutch like to say that their shrimp are tastier than wriggling pink rivals from the Far East.

In any event, like millions of other surnames that originated from occupations, the "Boll" name quite possibly got its origins from a "bolship," a type of fisherman's boat. The Dutch in earlier days used just nicknames to refer to one another, but at some point, according to Friso's research, they were required to take an official family name. My clan's surname isn't mentioned in church records until 1780, and then it is spelled "Bol."

With a family occupation so tied to the uncertainties of the sea, it was little surprise that Mother Nature would play an important role in the fortunes of the Boll family at some point. And in 1897, after shrimp fishing in Zoutkamp hit a long slump, my paternal grandfather, Johannes Bol, sailed his boat northeast along the coast, to Rysum, Germany—like Zoutkamp a fishing town, just west of the city of Emden. There, he met and married Henderiene Elkes, a local girl, in a medieval church.

My father, Anton, was born to Johannes and Henderiene on September 4, 1904, their fifth child. He was baptized in a church in nearby Campen, according to family records. By 1905, Johannes Boll had moved his growing brood to the bigger city of Emden, and two more children would follow. His occupation was listed as "dredger."

Within twenty years, according to Friso's research, the Boll family moved to Wolthusen, then a small town, now a suburb of

Emden, and were living at Ligariusstreet number 7, on the first floor. The family's livelihood was still tied to the sea. My grandfather's occupation sequentially was listed as "owner of a ship" in 1925, as "captain" in 1927, as "skipper" in 1934, and, by 1937, as "retired," according to the Emden Adressbook.

Meanwhile, my mother, Alberdiena Sekkur, was born in Zullen, north of Utrecht in the middle of the Netherlands, on November 1, 1904. In 1923, Friso's records show, Alberdiena's parents sold their ship. Then they owned a grocery store in Groningen, peddling potatoes and other vegetables, buying just enough each day from wholesalers because refrigeration wasn't yet available.

Although it isn't exactly known when my parents first connected, Friso's research suggests the future bride and groom knew each other from childhood because of their families' connections to the seafaring Groningen region, and perhaps from being together in school.

⌐⌐⌐⌐⌐

But that doesn't mean it was smooth sailing between my future parents, or at least between their families. As with so many couples, there was a star-crossed aspect to their relationship because of their lineage.

By the late 1800s, the Boll family was known as ship owners, with captains and other staff working for them. Their vessels were called "coasters," and sailed the Baltic Sea, off the coasts of Scandinavia and northern Germany, according to Friso's research. My grandfather owned three big ships, each about 300 feet long, large enough to transport commodities such as lumber and coal from Sweden to Europe's growing industrial centers.

By contrast, the Sekkur family owned just a single small boat and could only sail the inland waterways, not the Baltic or, especially, the highly exposed and near-Arctic waters of the North Sea.

This disparity in industry prominence and financial heft came to weigh heavily on my parents as their relationship blossomed. My grandmother, Henderiene Boll, was none too happy that her son and the Sekkur girl had taken a liking to each other, Friso discovered, partly because of the difference in the families' statuses. In fact, in the future, my grandmother would refuse to stay with my father and my mother's parents in Utrecht when the couple returned from the United States to visit, according to family legend.

My father was both a dreamer and a planner—that applied to his head and to his heart—and I'm certain he planted those same traits in me throughout my childhood. In the Dutch tradition, my grandfather helped his son get started in a trade, so my father began working in a bicycle shop. When he was eighteen years old, one of his customers was going to America, which piqued his interest. He ended up accepting the man's invitation to accompany him overseas. My father landed in Port Huron, Michigan, about an hour's drive north of Detroit along the St. Clair River at the bottom of Lake Huron, working odd jobs for several years and learning some English.

Still, my father never forgot about my mother. In fact, even before embarking for America the first time, it was clear in his mind that eventually he would marry her. Dutch law required presentation of two legitimate birth certificates for marriage, and my father made a copy of his birth certificate in March 1923—more than five years before he ultimately would marry her.

Friso's research shows my father went to America because he "saw opportunities for the future." In fact, she believes that my father was mainly "looking for adventure" when he soon departed Holland for America for good.

That information lines up with the stories I heard my parents tell over the years. For my dad, before and after he arrived in the United States, it was always about the American dream. I don't know exactly why he accepted the invitation to come to America or why he decided to live here. I never asked him how he could walk away from his parents and his country and go to a different place, where he didn't know the native language and when he wasn't yet skilled in a trade. He must have had some kind of vision that caused him to take such a risk. Or maybe it was God's plan for him all along.

While the life of the Boll family in Holland was comfortable and secure, they were more inclined to live a quiet and simple lifestyle. My father wasn't interested in creating disorder, but he wanted greater opportunities for himself, his future wife, and their children—and that meant striving for something better, which had become synonymous with what immigrants were doing in America.

And because my mother, his hoped-for companion for adventure, was central to the future he envisioned, my father decided that during one of his return visits to his homeland, he would take her as his bride—and let the family chips fall where they may.

———————

It may have taken lots of convincing for my father to persuade his future wife to go along with his plan. When he asked for her hand in marriage in the spring of 1928, each was only twenty-three years old. He had five brothers at home in addition to his parents, and she had two brothers and a sister as well as her folks. Despite my father's trips to America as a professional sailor, he had no acquaintances there, much less kin or good friends. They would be on their own.

It's lost to history whether their actions next were impulsive or long planned out, but while my father's copy of his birth certificate was getting wrinkled with years, my mother didn't apply for a copy of her birth certificate until June 9, 1928. Within three weeks, stunning their family members across the board, they got married. The next day, they were on that ship to the United States. Now, that's what I call eloping!

My father's initial plan, like that of so many immigrants who hopped off ships onto Ellis Island, was to find a job right where they'd landed, in New York. After all, Gotham not only was America's largest city, with a population of more than six million people, but it also was the most ethnically diverse, suggesting opportunity for just about anyone who came there and who was ambitious and determined enough to find work.

But my father's efforts to find a job were hampered by a number of factors, including his background as a sailor. The boroughs of New York City didn't have many jobs for seamen like him. Making matters worse, there wasn't a large, highly developed and cohesive Dutch community in the area like the enclaves of Italians, Irish, and other ethnic groups, who looked out for one another and hired their own.

My parents did somehow learn that they might want to look to Detroit for what they were seeking. Jobs in the developing auto industry were booming in Michigan as the Roaring Twenties were climaxing. Also, there were a lot of Dutch in the state; in fact, 150 miles to the west, in Grand Rapids, Michigan, a huge cluster of immigrants from Holland had formed a distinctive local community that was shaping the character of the entire west side of the state.

So my parents soon boarded a train to Detroit, where my father acquired a job as a tool-and-die apprentice in a factory. He worked for Midland Steel Company at its plant at the intersection of Van Dyke Road and 6-Mile Road in Detroit. Because my parents didn't have a car and my dad had to walk to work, they rented a house as close as they could to the factory. Their address was 7831 Sherwood Avenue, a location within a couple of miles of the old Midland plant—and one that now sits a few blocks away from the General Motors assembly plant straddling the border of Detroit and Hamtramck.

From the start in Michigan, my father was building for the future. The coming Great Depression would slow him down for a while as it did hundreds of millions of people the world over, but as a new decade dawned, he looked for ways to expand his income. He located a house with an unfinished upstairs and made a deal with the landlord: He'd finish off the attic himself, where he would make two sleeping rooms, and rent it out himself for some extra income. My parents preferred female renters who could be roommates, and there would be no drinking of alcoholic beverages allowed—nor gentleman visitors.

My father had plenty of reason to seek extra income and security—my mother was pregnant with their first child. I was born on June 20, 1929, just a few months before the stock market crash of October 1929. But the coming depression wouldn't stop my father, and nothing that happened in the half century to follow would slow me down, either.

CHAPTER 3
Apprentice at Life

I LEARNED SEVERAL IMPORTANT THINGS FROM my parents. Among them: the importance of sticking with decisions, the dividends of hard work, the vast potential in entrepreneurship, and the transcendent importance of faith. I would absorb and build on those lessons over the couple of decades I spent growing up in the Boll household.

As for my parents, they continued to defend their jarring decision to move to America the day after their wedding in Holland, despite all manner of complaining from their families over the years, and in the face of continual reminders how they'd abandoned their kin for an impulsive and selfish decision to move across the ocean to a country that no one from their homeland could afford to visit—especially during the Depression.

Of course, my parents empathized with their families' distress and certainly didn't want to cut off their deep ties to the Netherlands. After nearly a decade had passed, by the late 1930s, they were ready to revisit their homeland for the first time and introduce their two children to my grandparents. My sister, Diena, was born in 1930, just eleven months after me. My parents also finally had the financial wherewithal to do so, thanks to a decade of my father's hard work and scrappiness amid very challenging economic conditions.

They decided that my father would stay behind in Detroit and continue working, while my mother and us two kids would board a ship to Holland in May 1939. The plan was for my dad to take another ship in August and join us for the last couple of weeks of our visit, which would end in September.

There was a big problem with those plans, however. The winds of war in Europe had begun whipping wildly, as Adolph Hitler and the Nazis were gathering strength, and our extended vacation would head right into the vortex of the gathering storm. At the time, Hitler was threatening to attack Poland, and my family's plans included a stay in Emden, Germany, with my mother's parents.

Perhaps against their better judgment, my parents decided that we would still go as they had been planning the trip for many months. Back then, they didn't have the media and connectedness with the rest of the world that we do today, so I'm not sure my mother and father fully understood the dangers looming in Europe.

When we boarded a ship for the long trip to the Netherlands, I was nine years old. Diena remembers us sneaking from tourist class up to first class. Someone took a photo of my sister and me standing next to a "First Class" sign in the forbidden territory. "He was a rascal from the start," she said. "But it was indicative of the rest of his life: moving up from an ordinary, hard-working family to much, much better and bigger things."

Once in Europe, we stayed for several weeks with my father's parents in the Netherlands, and a much shorter time in Germany with my mother's folks. Her father by then was overseeing big construction jobs—in fact, he was helping set up factories where the Nazis would build three-person submarines that infamously targeted U.S. troop ships after America entered World War II.

I experienced the Germans' dislike of Americans firsthand—when I nearly lost my life on a lazy Sunday afternoon during our trip. Sunday was still very much the Sabbath day in Europe, with little going on outside of church, lunch, and rest. I celebrated my tenth birthday in Emden, and my grandparents gave me a toy sailboat as a present. So while still in my church clothes, I grabbed Diena's hand and we set out with a cousin for the local canal. As I set the little boat in the water, I lost my footing and fell into the water. I hadn't yet learned how to swim, so I scrambled wildly to pull myself out of the canal.

Fortunately, in a very timely way, a couple of local boys, seeing my distress, jumped in and helped me avoid drowning. Once I was safely on land, they asked me why I didn't speak fluent German. I told them it was because I was American. "If those boys had known that beforehand, they probably would have left him to drown," Diena remembered.

It saddened me that those German boys were already being taught to dislike Americans. Unfortunately, war-related hostilities would only get worse in a hurry. Nearing the end of that summer, not only did my father cancel his own plans to come to Holland, he also directed my mother to cut short our trip and return to America as quickly as we could. Thousands of other people wanted to leave Holland out of fears of a German invasion, and my mother struggled to get us tickets on a ship back to the U.S.

Finally, on September 6, 1939, five days after Germany invaded Poland and quickly advanced on Warsaw, my mother managed to secure our passage home. In response to Germany's aggression, England and France declared war on the Nazis, triggering World War II. My sister remembers that we were on the last boat out of Amsterdam. When we finally arrived home to the U.S., my father drove to New York to pick us up at the harbor. We couldn't get off the ship for several hours, however, until after we went through the required security inspections, which anyone arriving from Europe was subjected to.

The Netherlands had hoped to remain neutral during the great European conflict, but that was impossible once the Nazis invaded Holland on May 10, 1940. My parents' homeland fell in only five days and was occupied by Germans for the next five years. My relatives and their friends were forced from their homes, starved, and subjected to working in factories to support the Nazi war effort.

Despite my father's middling income from the factory, and his deep concerns about what his family was enduring in Europe, he guided our family through the Depression in relatively good shape. He sold the house near Hamtramck and bought another one a little farther north in the mid-1930s. "Maybe it was because Mom and Dad knew how to save," said Diena, "but it seemed like our house was always the one that had a big pot of soup going and everyone shared in it."

Along with having the discipline to save, my dad applied his self-taught construction skills to others' needs by fixing houses for money, and we all pitched in. It was ten years of very difficult times, but everyone helped one another. I think that's what helped Americans get to the other side of those very lean economic times. We'd go over to our friend Joe's house and build a room. Then people would socialize out on their porches, hanging over the rails and chatting. Most everyone got along back then because everyone was hurting, and we were all helping one another. I wish we had more of that nowadays.

Finally, after so many years of hard work, my dad was ready to purchase his next house. Shortly after returning from our trip to Holland in 1939, he decided we were going to leave Detroit and move into a nicer cottage in St. Clair Shores.

Of course, the price was right because the cottage had no heat—which was less than ideal during those bitterly cold, long Michigan winters. Dad's plan was to excavate under the house for a basement where he could install a furnace so that we could move in by the winter of 1940. I was old enough to help Dad dig dirt out from under the house, and, of course, we got other people to help us. We put house jacks underneath and removed dirt all summer. Then we put footings down with a mixer, gravel, and cement bags and hired someone to lay blocks for the foundation. Eventually, we lowered the house down and had a basement—and heat!

Unfortunately, the house had no fan system to distribute the warmth, so Diena and I spent many frigid nights sleeping in the attic. In an ill-advised attempt to keep my feet warm, I placed a reading lamp at the end of my bed. One night, the bulb caught the mattress on fire. Thankfully, we were able to put the fire out before it caused too much damage.

Helping my father as a kid was how I learned about building houses. I was just a little guy who couldn't do much but stand around and watch, but I did learn. And later, as I went to school, I met kids whose fathers were plumbers, carpenters, electricians, or other tradesmen. They weren't licensed, but they were able to thread a pipe or make a faucet work. They all helped one another back then, so I was able to learn a lot while just watching them work.

We had been living in the St. Clair Shores home for a couple of years by the time my parents welcomed their third child, my sister Henderiene, who would become known as "Riene." She was born in 1942. By then, my dad's plan was to build a diner on a lot near Lakeview High School in nearby Roseville, in Macomb County, while still keeping his factory job. There were no high-school cafeterias in those days, so he saw a great opportunity to feed students, teachers, and others who lived near the school. Unfortunately, World War II delayed his plans because it was almost impossible to get a construction license in that era, given the importance of conserving resources for the war effort.

But eventually my father got the clearance to build his diner and called it the Lighthouse. I was almost a teenager by then, so I was able to pitch in with the construction. Over the next couple of years, Diena and I helped the family business in other ways. By the time we were twelve or thirteen years old, we washed dishes in the evenings. I also helped keep the place clean and peeled potatoes, and Diena worked as a waitress. Our mother was the chef. "On Saturday night," Diena said, "we would get to turn the jukebox way up. It was a fun time, but a working time. The whole family worked together."

It wasn't long before my father's ambitions took his eye even further out into the suburbs and to a bigger enterprise, even though he would still have to moonlight to make it work. In 1948, he built a restaurant he would call the Light Tower, at 14-Mile and Gratiot Roads, decidedly far from Detroit at the time. He wanted to launch a more upscale establishment than his diner—moving up to, say, plates of roast beef and mashed potatoes from hamburgers. And he wanted to add rooms for travelers to stay over. Our family also would use a tiny apartment that he attached to the motel.

After World War II ended, it wasn't easy to get workers to travel so far from downtown Detroit. Some decided they would prefer to stay over during the week, instead of commuting back and forth. My dad realized pretty quickly that he was doing better renting rooms than with making dinners, so he converted part of the restaurant dining area into even more rental rooms.

———————

Faith was a very important part of my family's life. My father read the Bible to us every evening after dinner for fifteen to twenty minutes, in Dutch. On Sunday afternoons, aside from the occasional drive into the country, we sang hymns together, with my mother playing piano, my dad plucking a mandolin, and me stroking a violin that I had found time to learn. After we moved to St. Clair Shores, with no Dutch Reform congregation in the area, we started attending a Presbyterian church. My family also took on the job of maintaining the church, including cleaning up the rice after Saturday-afternoon weddings.

In fact, many years later, I made a donation to pay for that church's announcements sign on the front lawn as a memorial to my late mother, and to this day I have remained committed to covering whatever expenses Lakeshore Presbyterian Church incurs for maintaining and upgrading my tribute to her.

My family was built, like most Dutch, on beliefs of integrity, respectfulness, acceptance, perseverance, reliability, self-discipline, and efficiency. These were characteristics my parents were taught and passed onto me—ones that would pay big dividends later in my life. As I was growing up, this collective personality, combined with the Dutch Reform tradition of Protestantism, meant that I did things in a certain way.

For instance, my parents were staunchly conservative when it came to some social practices that had become part of the twentieth-century landscape in mainstream America. One of them was alcohol consumption. Another was dancing. Both were verboten in the Reform tradition and in adherent households.

My parents winked a bit at some sectarian prohibitions, such as consuming alcohol. Dad never drank, but it wasn't such a big no-no. Alcohol just wasn't something offered at our dinner table, while it was present in other ethnic traditions that were shaping the post-war generation. There was another reason my family was more conservative than others—liquor was expensive. It was a big thing to go to someone's house and have a beer, and I gradually evolved out of the no-drinking thing.

On the other hand, my parents were much stricter about something else: their dislike for Catholicism. When I was growing up, my father forbade us from dating Catholics. If I was seeing a girl, the first thing he'd do was find out if she was Catholic. Of course, I abided by my father's wishes over the years, but this rule became especially problematic for us when Diena insisted on getting serious with a Catholic guy.

One evening when she was about twenty years old and had persisted in dating the young man, Diena came home to see her bags packed and on the front steps of our house. While she would soon break up with the "infidel," and her rift with our parents didn't cause a lifetime of estrangement, it did become a significant factor in her path. When a physician my family knew offered to help Diena get into a medical technician program at a school in St. Louis, my alienated and ambitious sister packed up her own bags—and took off.

Higher education wasn't an option for me. After graduating from high school, my father informed me that college wasn't in the cards. We simply didn't have the money for me to go. My dad said, "Why don't you learn a trade?" I tried plumbing and became an apprentice for $1 an hour. I worked at it for about six months, but I wasn't learning anything.

I was seeking something else, and I guess that I was beginning to tap into the energy, ambition, and inventiveness that would prove to be accelerants throughout the rest of my life. I quit the plumbing gig and went to work, for $2.25 an hour, at a Chrysler plant that was one of many in the Detroit area gearing up to supply new vehicles to returning GIs who were picking up their lives, building families and careers.

Initially I worked as a metal finisher. I filed down and smoothed out a weld line on a vehicle and was assigned to do the task on every eighth car; others would take their turns on the other seven coming down the line. As a younger guy, I was fast enough and strong enough to do all eight cars, but other guys would get mad at me. Most importantly, the union didn't want me to make it obvious that the job didn't require eight men!

Soon I figured out how to profit from my efficient ways and excess energy. I also landed a job on the line of a nearby Hudson plant, working a second shift that began at three in the afternoon. To help me get through the drudgery, I found a way to job-share with another guy on the Hudson line. We would each do every fourth car and would keep the line going. He would sleep in the locker room, and when he came down to take my place, I'd go sleep in the same hideaway. Of course, we had no time to spend all our money because we were working six days a week.

Among other advantages of leaving everything I could muster out on the factory floor in those days, I cleared enough money to buy a car, on which I had to make payments of $80 a month. Again, a foundation I had laid earlier would help me get through the next phase of life.

The U.S. Army drafted me for the Korean War in 1951 just as my father was expanding the Light Tower into a larger motel. I took basic training in South Carolina, transferred to Fort Sam Houston in San Antonio for training as a medic, and then was sent back to Fort Bragg for maneuvers. As I said earlier, I obtained permission from the Army to park my car on base. That was crucial because a lot of guys in the Army needed rides back home, including to Michigan. I would charge them each $30 and take them home for the weekend. That left my pay as an Army private, which also amounted to about $80 a month, free for other uses.

Soon the 1949 Mercury I bought also would come in handy for another important task.

CHAPTER 4
Sealing the Deal

MARLENE'S SERENDIPITOUS ENCOUNTER WITH me in 1951 was only the latest major development in her life. She was born on February 20, 1933, in Roselle, New Jersey, into a Brady Bunch kind of family. Her father, Frank Miller, was a widower with three children, and her mother, born Lina Fuchs, by that time was a widow with two children of her own. After the families combined, Marlene came along as the first—and last—offspring of both of her parents, blending her father's German ancestry with her mother's roots in France.

More than for many people, Marlene's position in the family's birth order would become an important aspect of her life. "By the time I was born, one of my sisters already had gotten married," she recalled. "And as time went on, other siblings got married as well. So I was almost brought up as an only child."

The Millers were living in a two-bedroom, one-bath bungalow in Roselle when she was born. The Great Depression already had taken a toll on the family, with the sudden collapse of the economy dooming Frank's company. In the wake of that crushing blow, her father found a job as head of maintenance for the school district's five buildings in Roselle, New Jersey.

Even as a little girl, Marlene turned to dancing and music as outlets for creative play and to help fill emotional gaps as she coped with being an only child in the household. "Dad looked at me pretty strangely at times as I danced around the house, because he was conservative," Marlene remembered. "But early on, I asked to start taking dance lessons. And I prevailed."

Not only was dancing a key to Marlene's mental health and well-being, soon it would come in handy for other reasons. Her father died in 1949 when she was 16 years old. And though her family had recovered from the Great Depression, and Marlene had been their only dependent, her re-widowed mother would soon lean on her daughter financially.

"We had limited funds and no income," Marlene recalled. "The house was paid for, but I felt I had to get jobs on the weekends for extra money for us. One thing I did was make venetian blinds. But there were some nights when we had to eat rabbit stew."

Fortunately, in early 1950, when Marlene was a junior in high school, the Roxy Theater in New York was holding auditions for a dance troupe it called "The Roxyettes"—a high-kicking chorus line—which would tour state fairs and other venues in Canada and on the U.S. East Coast that summer. She made the cut and enjoyed life on the road with a couple dozen other girls, as well as the feeling of independence and adventure it gave her.

She entered her senior year of high school with lots of joy and confidence. Marlene was becoming a self-sufficient woman, filling her life with dance. After school hours, she gave dance lessons to little girls in exchange for advanced instruction for her by the studio owner. She also eagerly signed up again for The Roxyettes for the summer of 1951, for a similar East Coast tour. If she completed the tour again after graduating from high school, she figured it would be easier for her to get a job in New York when she returned.

Once Marlene and I agreed to write to each other after the end of The Roxyettes' tour in Charlotte in August 1951, I had a big problem: I hadn't been straight with my new girlfriend about exactly what I was doing in the Carolinas. As I mulled over my very real feelings for this girl, I concluded that the innocent fib we had told the six dancers suddenly loomed much larger than a little white lie.

Sure, I could fool anyone for a few hours by spewing medical jargon and pretending to be in training as a doctor, which is exactly what my buddies and I had done with Marlene and the other Roxyettes during two weekends on leave. Yet as I began to think that I might get serious about Marlene, I had to figure out some way to tell her the truth.

But not right away. Part of the deal from the start was that my buddy Pete also was in on the tall tale because he had taken a liking to Melva and promised to write to her, just as Marlene and I had vowed to exchange letters with each other.

Here was the biggest problem: Having told our stories to the girls, where were we going to have them write to? Fortunately, I had a friend in Columbia who was married and allowed to live off base, so he let Pete and me use his address and give it to the girls. That's where their letters back to us would go, which solved one problem. Another dilemma: When Pete and I wrote to them, we had to make sure our stories were alike, about what we were doing in "medical school" and so on, because of course the girls were talking about their letters from us.

After much thought, I decided, for better or worse, that I was going to unravel my masquerade gradually rather than tell Marlene the entire truth abruptly. It might have been too much for her to take. It helped that in the meantime, Pete and Melva had lost interest in each other and weren't corresponding anymore. I now was in complete control of what Marlene was learning about me.

So I told another white lie. In a letter, I explained to Marlene that I'd been drafted and was leaving college to go back to Michigan; that at least got me "into the Army," in her mind. But I complicated my story by telling her that, of all places, the Army was yanking me back from Michigan and stationing me at Fort Jackson—in Columbia.

To help pull off this ruse, I wrote to my mother back home and told her that a letter would be coming from this lady addressed to me, and so would you please put it in an envelope and send it on to me at Fort Bragg. I figured Mom wouldn't know what the heck was going on, so it would work. If nothing else, at least now I was writing to Marlene as a soldier.

While Marlene had no inkling about what her new boyfriend actually was doing, I wasn't exactly the center of her life at that point. Literally on the heels of her two successful summer tours with The Roxyettes and her growing devotion to dance as a career, Marlene was coming into her own as a Roxyette. She won dancing jobs backing up talent such as Frankie Lane and Marilyn Monroe at The Roxy Theater.

And then a friend, the Roxyettes' choreographer, got Marlene a slot on *The Ed Sullivan Show* along with seven other girls. She appeared on the same stage where Elvis Presley, the Beatles, and many other acts would make famous appearances on what was back then must-see TV on Sunday nights. Before ending its run in 1971, Ed Sullivan ranked as one of the few entertainment shows to have aired in the same weekly time slot on the same network for more than two decades.

Marlene enjoyed the Ed Sullivan performances as a sort of apprenticeship in the upper reaches of the dance world. But after about a year and a half, she gladly left the TV show for what she considered her dream job: as a Rockette, dancing on the already-legendary stage of Radio City Music Hall in front of live audiences only. She nailed an audition to become one of thirty-six Rockettes who were employed doing their high-kicking stuff at any one time. Each Rockette would work for four weeks straight and then have a week off, and there would be ten on vacation at any one time—with twenty-four, plus two more girls to cover illnesses, on stage every weekend.

"It was grueling, but I loved it," Marlene said. "I lived in New Jersey with my mom, and I would commute back and forth. I'd get up at 5 a.m. every day for 7 o'clock rehearsals, and we'd do four shows each day—and five on weekends."

⌒

By then, it had been about a year and a half since we'd left each other in a parking lot in Charlotte. I went to San Antonio for further training as a medic. At one point I was also shipped to San Francisco, where I was pulled out of line to get on a ship to go to war. Instead, I eventually helped oversee preparations for soldiers who were going to be transported to South Korea. I was put in charge of a ferry that carried soldiers to those ships.

A lot of these soldiers were eighteen and nineteen years old and never had left home, and here they were being put on troop ships to go across the Pacific. Of course, many became nauseated with seasickness and suffered headaches from fear and anxiety, and I was the guy on board assigned to take care of them. I asked my Army superiors what I should give them. They handed me a bottle that contained aspirin. They told me, "Just don't tell them." As long as the boys were taking something, the Army figured, they would settle down.

Even though Marlene and I were now living on opposite ends of the U.S., we were still going strong through our letters. I'll admit that I did nothing to dispel the fabrications I had told her early on; medical school and becoming a doctor were still part of how I presented myself in writing. I knew my situation would become even more complicated once my military commitment ended. The war in Korea had been at a stalemate for nearly two years as the sides talked peace and maintained a ceasefire. In advance of an armistice that would be signed in July 1953, I was discharged from the Army along with thousands of other American troops who had remained stateside. In February 1953, I was allowed to go home.

Now the clock was ticking on my made-up biography because, naturally, Marlene expected we'd be able to see each other again soon. And our discussions about our relationship had reached the possibility of getting engaged. I went back to Michigan and called her, and we agreed that I would come to New York to see her in April. I felt at this point I couldn't carry on my story any longer and that it was time for me to end the charade and tell her everything.

During the 600-mile drive in my Mercury to the Millers' doorstep in Roselle, I swallowed hard and went over in my mind how I would come clean to Marlene. After I'd spent about a year and a half dispensing falsehoods in my letters to her, I knew it would be hard for Marlene to believe I'd simply made everything up. I also knew that it might be very difficult for her to forgive me—even though I wanted her more than ever to become my wife. During that long drive, I feared that in only a matter of hours, I might be further from that goal than ever.

After an emotional reunion, I settled in for what was supposed to be a visit of several days. The next day, I took the train with

Marlene into Manhattan and attended a couple of Rockettes shows—waving my white handkerchief from one of the front rows as I had during her performances in North Carolina in the summer of 1951. When we went out to dinner in the city that evening, I gulped—the awful moment had arrived.

First, I talked vaguely about engagement and getting married. But then I pivoted to the unpleasant truth I had to share with her before such discussions could go any further. Slowly, I went through it all with her, and at first she didn't believe me—or didn't want to believe me. So then I took out a photo album and showed her pictures of me in my Army uniform from the period when we'd met.

Looking in her eyes, I told her in a soft but assured voice that it was something she needed to think about, and ultimately decide whether it was something she could forgive me for. I certainly hoped she would. My strategy was not to force anything or pressure her. I just said that I knew she may need some time to think about this, and I would call her in a few days. I was going to stay in a motel near her house for a couple of days, just to make it easier on her.

But as someone who'd been good at thinking on his feet even as a kid, I soon decided not to let our future together sit solely in Marlene's lap. I could still wield some influence on her decision, even without talking directly to her. While she was busy each day working in the city, I would drop by her house and help her mother with tasks, many of which had needed completion for years. I fixed her broken drawers and painted the inside of the house. I wrapped a rag around my head and face and painted away. I was very fast. By the time Marlene and I got our heads together again, I had much of the inside of the house painted and repaired.

As for what Marlene was thinking about us, I was disappointed to learn that I wasn't the only thing—or suitor—on her mind. She had been working too hard to discuss the situation with her closest friends. "It wasn't my highest priority," she said. "I couldn't believe I'd been snowed. But then as I was thinking about it, I would look down past the orchestra pit and didn't see anybody waving a white hankie. At the same time, I was getting calls from this young man who went to school with me and who I would date occasionally."

Marlene thought and prayed about it for three days. "Despite everything, I focused on the fact that there was just something about John," she said. "He was always there. He had always been writing letters. He was very kind. You don't meet people like that every day."

And Marlene got extra encouragement from an unexpected source—her mother, who agreed that while I pulled one over on her, I was a "nice guy."

Finally, with my heart nearly racing through my chest, Marlene told me, "I think we can work something out.'"

Naturally, getting married to Marlene wasn't as simple as moving past the big fib I'd told just to get to the starting line with her. The finish line remained well in the distance. We had to spend time together, get each other's families acclimated to our partnership, and start to figure out the rest of our lives.

Marlene's situation was by far the more complicated. I felt strongly that I could build a great life for us once we were back in Detroit. But Marlene's budding career as a professional dancer really could only flourish in one place: New York City. Giving up that possibility, to try to find something on the same scale elsewhere, would be like asking a bullfighter to leave Mexico or a palace guard to leave Buckingham. Was it really fair for me to ask her to leave Broadway? Also very important was the fact that Marlene was her mother's biggest means of financial support.

Other potential complications clouded the picture too. For instance, our mismatching faiths could prove a problem.

Marlene wasn't Catholic—but her dad had been a staunch Methodist, often serving as a Scripture reader during Sunday services. And it was pretty clear that Dutch Reform was a way of life in my family. If she joined my church in Michigan, she might well become the only professional dancer in the entire world of Dutch Reformed.

"This was a major decision for me, because Mom was alone, and I was taking care of her financially and leaving a job I'd worked very hard for," Marlene said. "And I was pretty close to my siblings, though they were all spread around. So we had to discuss it at length."

Already a skilled closer, I was able to seal this particular deal by vowing to Marlene that, if we were married, I would take care of her mother—I'd do whatever necessary for her to live a happy life.

"Trust me," I implored her, once more.

And, thankfully for me, she did.

After all of that, the next step was just putting our plan to marry in action—although not without its own drama. One such moment came in the fall of 1953, when Marlene finally would meet my family in Michigan as she traveled there for an engagement party. She flew from Newark, New Jersey, to City Airport in Detroit and waited for the plane to roll down the tarmac to an area where, back then, anyone could come and greet an arriving flight and gather at the bottom of the stairs.

Marlene was dressed, stunningly, in a white lace dress and high heels, with her blonde locks flowing from underneath a dainty hat. To everyone in Michigan who'd never laid eyes on Marlene, it might as well have been the scandalous Marilyn Monroe or a curvy Betty Grable herself emerging from the door of that plane. She might as well have hopped down the stairs dressed like a June Taylor dancer—or a Rockette. And during her descent, she couldn't help but demonstrate a bit of the graceful prance she'd learned on stage.

"It was traumatic for me," Marlene said. "Here I was getting off the airplane looking like this, and John's family was all arranged in a semicircle at the bottom of the stairs, dressed very conservatively as they did. I thought they were Amish. I was very surprised, and I certainly couldn't read their faces. I looked at them and thought maybe I ought to get back on the plane and go home."

But it took only seconds for Marlene to evolve, at least in my family's view, from a glamorous and celebrity-like curiosity to just being a part of the family. In fact, she probably had been spared a more shocked reaction because the Boll women had seen her dance on *The Ed Sullivan Show*. So despite the women's doubts about Marlene on paper, in the flesh, "They took me in right away," Marlene said. "I felt very comfortable with them."

We danced over the last hurdle, and Marlene and I were going to get married with the blessings of everyone who mattered to us. We planned for a wedding the next year, with Marlene getting rides from friends to check out various wedding venues in Roselle and surrounding areas. Ultimately, we chose the little Methodist church in which she'd grown up.

I went to New Jersey a few weeks early and performed another round of renovations on her mother's house before all the company would come by for the wedding, painting the living room and dining room and generally sprucing up the place for her and Marlene. And on June 19, 1954, on the last day of spring, we became John and Marlene Boll.

CHAPTER 5

A Wheelbarrow and a Shovel

GETTING IN ON THE EXPANSION OF THE DETROIT suburbs in the 1950s was like trying to ride a tiger. But I was determined to climb onto the beast anyway.

By 1950, fueled by a half-century boom in the auto industry, Detroit had become the fourth-largest city in America with a population that reached 1.85 million as individuals streamed from all over the country to find work at the General Motors, Ford, and Chrysler plants and rooted themselves in nearby neighborhoods. Over those fifty years, Detroit was one of the fastest-growing core cities in the country with an expansion pace exceeded only by that of Los Angeles among the nation's twenty largest cities. At the same time, Detroit's ring of suburbs on the north, west, and south was growing robustly as well. All told, the metro area's 1950 population of nearly 3.2 million was six times that of the region in 1900.

But as I settled into my new life with Marlene, we also were on the cusp of a new trend, one we both exemplified—and benefited from. For by the early 1950s, the city of Detroit proper actually had reached a zenith to which it never would return. Auto production in the city peaked in 1955, partly because residents of tight-knit neighborhoods began to resist the imposition of even more factories in their backyards by eminent domain. Meanwhile, automation eliminated many of the remaining car plant jobs that had drawn and kept people in Detroit in the first place.

Members of the city's middle class were leaving as an underclass—less capable and seemingly less interested in continuing to make the Motor City shine—took their place.

By the mid-1950s Detroit's suburbs were becoming huge beneficiaries of some of the same dynamics that were hurting the main urban hub. After all, Americans were still buying cars in record numbers even though the traditional workforce in the Motor City no longer was benefiting as much from the continued boom. The Greatest Generation was still bearing their "Baby Boomer" kids, and the U.S. government was building the nationwide interstate highway system—and both developments were going to demand a lot more automobiles.

But now blue- and white-collar workers in the auto industry were leaving Detroit for nearby suburbs such as Ferndale, Oak Park, Harper Woods, and Dearborn, where Ford Motor completed its mammoth "Glass House" headquarters building in 1956. Some residents were flocking to towns even farther away, such as Taylor, Livonia, and Royal Oak, because new auto plants were following them outside Detroit proper.

St. Clair Shores, of course, was where my parents had ended up in the late 1940s after starting in Detroit in 1928, and growth was sprouting up around them—and their Light Tower restaurant and hotel in nearby Roseville. Soon I would be doing more than my part to ensure the Macomb County boom continued.

Leaning on what I'd learned from doing construction work with my father since I was a little boy, and on my proven engineer-like penchant for breaking things down so I understood how to build them up again, I entered the construction business after my discharge from the Army in 1952.

I knew one thing: I didn't want to go back to the factory. I liked the outdoors and I thought if I got a job in construction, I could learn more about how to build a house and get more experience. Through friends, I obtained a spot with an underground-utility contractor in nearby Mount Clemens for $2 an hour. My employer was one of the firms that had jumped on the opportunity to excavate gas, water, and sewer lines that utility companies and municipalities were installing to keep up with the influx of people into Detroit's northern suburbs. It was a pretty rough job because I was digging pretty deep. Looking back now, I know that I could have gotten hurt. Nonetheless, I would later realize how fortunate I was to learn the construction trade from the ground up.

On evenings and weekends in 1954, even before Marlene and I were married, I went to work building our first house. With

$300 in savings, I purchased a lot in Roseville near 12-Mile Road where I would construct our first home at 29875 Park Street. It had one floor, which was a popular design at the time, with three bedrooms. At first, I didn't even tell Marlene that I was building our house. I really can't recall why—maybe I wanted it to be a wedding surprise.

I only remember that there were four of us who were buddies, and we helped one another build all our houses. Over several weeks, we dug the basement, erected the outside walls, and installed a roof, so by our wedding day, the house was closed in. Eventually I told Marlene that I was building a home for us, but I still didn't give her any idea what it looked like. She was back in New Jersey, so she couldn't see how it was coming.

After the wedding and a quick honeymoon in Myrtle Beach, South Carolina, we loaded up the Mercury with all of the belongings and wedding gifts Marlene could fit into it—including a bunch of things we secured to the car's roof —and headed for Detroit with our $25 in savings. When we pulled up to 29875 Park, Marlene remembered, "I was shocked. The house was almost bigger than the one I grew up in. It was a surprise to me that he had that kind of talent."

We stayed in a unit at my father's motel for a couple of months until I could finish our house. My sister, Diena, and her husband, Gene Nelson, also lived at the motel by then, and to help earn their keep, Diena and Marlene worked side by side as maids, washing sheets and cleaning toilets.

Meanwhile, I continued my day job and worked with my saw in the basement at Park Street whenever I could, painstakingly finishing doors and building my own kitchen cabinets. I even laid the tile. Our home was quite spartan at first. "We didn't have any furniture except a kitchen table and couch that they sent over from the motel," Marlene said. "We didn't know the difference. We were having a good time."

Not that all was rosy. Marlene would plant flowers outside our new bungalow, she said, "And [I'd] say to myself, is this really what I wanted to be doing?" In hindsight, it was just the case of two people getting to know each other—and marriage. We had to learn to live together, and like everyone, we had likes and dislikes. All of those things were new for us.

As a couple, we fell in with some of my old friends and their wives. None of us was that well off. In fact, my work with a small construction company remained unpredictable, so Marlene looked for a dance-related opportunity. She was more than happy to do it. "I couldn't keep my feet still for long," she said.

There were some dance opportunities in Detroit, she said, but the city's entertainment scene "was very new. I went to a couple of auditions and didn't care for them; it wasn't like New York. I ended up teaching at a dance school in East Detroit, but they really didn't have the proper facilities for dancers; they had concrete floors."

Marlene persisted in earning a paycheck in part because I soon got laid off as a post-Korean War lull hit the economy and development slowed for a while. Never idle, I used some of the time to finish our basement and quickly crafted a dance studio for Marlene, including mirrors and exercise bars—and wood floors—where she could conduct her own school. With her top-shelf credentials and proper teaching setting, it wasn't long before she was shuffling eighty students in and out of that tiny basement and ranking as our family's breadwinner.

Meanwhile, I was constantly searching for odd jobs, accompanied only by a wheelbarrow and a shovel that I threw in the trunk of the Mercury. I would do anything to gain some traction, including back-breaking excavation work as well as cleanup at construction sites.

For a while, I specialized in hooking up homes on Jefferson Avenue in St. Clair Shores to sewer lines that were being newly dug by the city. It was painstaking work, but at least it was work. I would go down the street at about 5 o'clock in the evening because that's about when guys were returning home from their jobs. I hired a guy who owned a tractor to do the digging for me. I knew what had to be done for the hookups, but I wasn't a licensed plumber. So after a while, there was a certain inspector, named Mr. Williams, trying to find this "plumber" who was cheating. It was me he was chasing.

As the economy improved, I had a better choice in jobs and more work. We managed to save an astounding $1,000 over the next several months. Determined to go out on my own and not have to rely on others for work, I used the money to buy a tractor with a backhoe and a loader so I could take on bigger jobs. Quickly I also was able to hire a man named Lot Murray who had migrated to Detroit from Mississippi in search of work. Murray became my right-hand man in 1955, and he would end up working for us for the next thirty-five years, including a primary role of giving my mother-in-law rides to run errands. Eventually, he ended up serving fifteen years as the caretaker of our future home in Grosse Pointe. He was such a great man and trusted friend. He was part of our family.

Harnessing my determination and tireless energy, I kept building my enterprise, which I called Prescott Excavating. Soon my payroll rose to about a half-dozen people, with Marlene relying on her high-school accounting skills to keep the books for my company as well as run her dance studio.

Soon a paving contractor and one of my sometime customers, Western Construction, came to me and promised that if I would invest in proper excavating equipment, the company would guarantee me two years of work as it tried to keep up with the pace of commercial and residential development in Macomb. I advised them that I didn't have money or equipment but that I could try to find a couple of other guys and, together, we could do something like that.

I knew two brothers, Chuck and John Trombley from our Lakeview High School days, who also were in the construction business. And they already owned a crane, a bulldozer, and some other equipment. Named for our alma mater, Lakeview Excavating was born. Together we were now able to take on larger jobs.

Indeed, with more and bigger equipment, a bigger company, and bigger capabilities, I was starting to rub shoulders with my bigger future—and some bigger people. In turn, Lakeview Excavating began to get a big reputation.

Take Eli Broad, for example. In *Forbes* magazine's list of the richest Americans for 2020, the Detroit native was ranked #216, with a fortune estimated at about $7 billion. With its roots in the same Macomb County mud where I was toiling, his Kaufman & Broad company became one of the nation's largest home builders, supplying parents of Baby Boomers with affordable site housing; then he created the annuities giant SunAmerica.

But back in 1954, Eli Broad was just a recent product of Michigan State University and a freshly minted accountant—albeit a cum laude graduate of the school and one of the youngest CPAs ever approved in the state of Michigan. He was even teaching night classes in accounting at the Detroit Institute of Technology by 1956.

Broad also began working with a brother-in-law, Donald Kaufman, who was building "stick homes" in Macomb County. Donald was a guy who played around on airplanes on the weekends and was a glider pilot. I wasn't sure I wanted to get involved with Kaufman—we didn't have much in common—but Eli came to me and said he wanted to develop a particular block in Warren at 10-Mile and Schoenherr roads. He didn't have any seed money, so he needed me to carry him at the beginning of a project that was going to end up costing many millions of dollars.

I was aware of the risk; at that early point in my career, it would only have taken one bad job to put me under. But I spoke to many people who knew both Broad and Kaufman, and we agreed to do the job based on their recommendations. My understanding was that we weren't going to get paid for months. But Eli paid me—in fact, he paid me way ahead of time.

And with that, he rewarded me with their next job. We ended up doing all of their excavating in the City of Warren and all of their construction up Van Dyke as they managed to buy up farms.

Because of my faith in him, Broad favored me in return. That's the kind of thing that allowed us to build our company and grow our network.

As my company began to take off working with Kaufman & Broad and other new customers, there remained huge, unfinished business in our family. Marlene and I were about to expand our household, in more ways than one.

CHAPTER 6

A Houseful

MARLENE AND I ENJOYED THE FUN OF BUILDING our nest for two while working hard in our chosen vocations, which allowed us to begin enjoying some of life's spoils. For example, in 1956, I was able to scratch an itch from my childhood and buy my first boat, a twenty-one-foot "kit" vessel that I pieced together myself. We also took up skiing on local hills and in northern Michigan as a hobby, together and with some friends. While my lankiness and coordination allowed me to pick up the sport easily, Marlene's natural grace and athleticism made her look like she was snow dancing when she put on her skis.

After five years of marriage, we also were beginning to long for more, and eager to get on with some of the major unfinished business of our lives together: addressing the needs of Marlene's mother, building our own family, and moving into a more spacious home in the suburbs. Those would be our priorities as the decade drew to a close.

————————

At our first house in Roseville, Marlene and I loved gathering family members and friends for games, barbecues, and Sunday afternoon get-togethers. Depending on how many people showed up, these occasions were sometimes tight fits. As I expanded Lakeview Excavating with the Trombley brothers, I began searching for a larger home that would afford us the space to grow a family and entertain friends. Fortunately, because of the surge in development north of Detroit, the value of our house on Park Street roughly doubled in just a few years.

And because of my excavation work, I was able to scout out potential locations in and around Macomb County before almost everyone else. Marlene would accompany me on some scouting trips, and we began eyeing a vacant site in the growing community of Fraser, in semi-rural Clinton Township, that sat beside the Clinton River. It was about four miles to the northeast of Park Street. The home site was a lovely and quiet place.

Over the next several months, we designed and built a three-bedroom ranch home that would give us all the room we needed to expand our lives and our household. I helped oversee its construction. At one point, I ordered a bricklayer to tear down a nearly completed wing wall on the front of the house because it looked a bit crooked to me. I wanted our home to be perfect. After several months of construction, we moved into our new house in August 1960.

The best part of our new home was a huge, rectangular in-ground pool in the back, which was surrounded by a wide concrete deck. The pool was perched on an eight-foot-high wall that gave us a commanding view of the lawn that sloped away behind it, sprinklings of trees, and the Clinton River flowing east to Lake St. Clair. I hung a long rope swing on a stout branch of one of the sturdiest trees so kids would be able to soar out over the river in glee.

A few years later, our pool would become such a local attraction that we struck a deal with the YMCA to give kids—including our children—swimming instruction there. We had to provide certain safety features and it was theirs to use.

Unfortunately, there was an unforeseen hazard with our house that became apparent only years later. It fell victim to floods. The more the neighborhood was developed, the more our site was vulnerable to flooding. There was so much construction happening in that area that it began to create a lot more water flow to the Clinton River and to a drainage canal that ran through our property. The result was that the river and drains couldn't handle all the water that used to soak into the ground. Instead, it would run over the banks. If we got a hard rain, it would fill our entire backyard right up to the house.

For a long time, I was bringing a bulldozer home at night and on the weekends, trying to push dirt around so the property could handle the high water. It was a difficult situation, but we eventually got it figured out.

Marlene's aging mother, Lina, was never far from our minds. She had remained in the house in New Jersey, which I continued to repair and upgrade from time to time. I was steadily positioning myself to make good on my promise to Marlene that I would take care of her mother if she moved to Michigan to be with us.

With the move into our new home in Fraser, I finally could do exactly that. Marlene's five siblings all lived on the East Coast, but Marlene didn't feel Lina was receiving the kind of care and attention she needed and would be better off living with us. It was Marlene, after all, who had been Lina's primary provider since her father died when Marlene was sixteen. So after I handled the sale of her house in Roselle, Lina picked up stakes in New Jersey and moved into a new mobile home near us. She moved into our new house once it was finished.

Lina had extra reason for enjoying her move: the opportunity to babysit. Long wanting children but unable to conceive for more than five years, Marlene and I started talking about adoption. The state of Michigan had an agency that handled adoptions back then, so we made an application. As part of the requirements, we had to undergo physical examinations to make sure we were healthy enough to become parents. Marlene was fine, but the doctor called and said he wanted me to come back. That's when I learned that I had atrial fibrillation (AFib), which is a quivering or irregular heartbeat. Fortunately my case wasn't too bad—I've lived with the condition for more than sixty years—and it didn't prevent us from adopting.

We were put on a waiting list with other parents and waited several months until a child was available. One day in 1959, we got a call and were told to go to Lansing, Michigan, to meet a baby that we might like to adopt. It was a baby boy who was about six weeks old. His given name was Michael. We didn't know anything about his parents or the circumstances as to why he was given up for adoption; we were only told that he was born in Pennsylvania. We spent time with him, fell in love with him, and agreed to bring him home.

When Marlene and I introduced our new baby boy to my mother, she asked about his name. When we told her that he was named Michael, she immediately objected.

"No, he's Dutch," she told us. "His name is Janny."

So we named him John Jr.

Three years later, the state adoption agency called us again and informed us that they had a baby girl who needed a home.

Unfortunately, we couldn't take her right away because Marlene was dealing with a back injury; her back muscles had tightened up and were spasming, possibly due to her dancing. We waited about three months to adopt another beautiful child, whom we named Lora.

Then, miraculously, we had another daughter, Kristine, who was born to Marlene in 1965. I came home from work one evening, and Marlene was standing in our house in Fraser. She grabbed me, hugged me, and kissed me. "Guess what?" she said. "I'm pregnant!"

We were both so grateful for being able to adopt and now Marlene was expecting.

Grandma Miller made an easy fit with our family and her new life, which would extend for twenty-seven more years after she became part of our household. She took a special shine to John Jr. and me. And Lina loved what became her central role in caretaking in our home, where she variously cooked, cleaned, ironed, and watched the kids. Lina never learned to drive, so she couldn't participate in shuttling her grandchildren around to their various activities—but she was the steady presence in the house that allowed all the gears of our growing family to function properly.

We certainly needed the help back then. In the early days of our excavating company, I worked late and didn't come home until 8 o'clock at night. Marlene and her mother always had dinner waiting for me. Back then, I was driving large excavating machinery and working in the trenches, so I'd come home covered in mud. Marlene wouldn't let me in the house. She would hose me down in the garage, which wasn't too much fun in the winter, and the kids would be waiting for me in their pajamas at the fireplace.

Beyond all of this, Lina never asked for much specifically to be happy. She did insist on watching General Hospital every weekday afternoon at 3 o'clock; she also reliably enjoyed a bottle of beer at about 4 o'clock. Lina loved to be taken on an occasional shopping trip to downtown Detroit and to the Hudson's store, where she would pick up a hot dog and a Budweiser for lunch with her friends.

Our household was growing. But in the meantime, a tragic loss would rip away someone so dear to my family that we would never fully get over it.

CHAPTER 7

An Unspeakable Tragedy

AS MARLENE AND I EXPANDED OUR FAMILY, MY parents, Anton and Alberdiena Boll, continued to build their Light Tower Motel on Gratiot Road in Roseville. My father had retired from his career as a tool-and-die maker, and the motel was providing my parents with exactly what he planned: a reliable income and a slower pace in semi-retirement. And now he could provide my mother more help to operate the motel and restaurant instead of just handling expansion and maintenance.

Like any business venture, there were bumps along the road. In May 1951, while I was away in the Army and my sister, Diena, was studying in St. Louis, flames roared through the Light Tower, which at that point consisted mainly of a dining room with a few rooms for rent. And if not for a rescue by our family's faithful dog, the fire might have killed my youngest sister, Riene.

Only nine years old, Riene was watching television in the first small apartment-type unit that my dad had attached to the restaurant. Mom and Dad were in back in the garden where they were tending vegetables for the diner. Erica, our family's Doberman, began barking wildly as she reacted to flames that suddenly sparked a fire in the utility room, where she was nursing six puppies. Erica bounded into the living room, according to an account in the next day's *South Macomb News*, and tugged at Riene's dress, pulling her toward the outside door. At that point, my sister noticed the fire was raging in other parts of the building.

By the time local firefighters reached the site, according to the newspaper, "smoke and flames were spurting from every aperture of the building." Despite the work of sixty firemen, operating six pumpers and a tank truck for nearly two hours, the blaze totally gutted the Light Tower, causing what Dad estimated at the time was $30,000 in damages. It was "Roseville's worst loss in many years," the *News* said.

Fortunately my father had insurance on the property and would quickly rebuild the Light Tower into a thriving business. At that point, Dad decided he had enough land to transform the place into a motel where people could stay overnight or for a week with their car parked outside. He ended up making the new rooms apartment-like units with little kitchenettes. People would drive until midnight, see the "Vacant" sign, and peel off and make arrangements for a room or a unit.

But tragically for my family, at that site there would be a more devastating loss to come.

Almost a decade later, Mom and Dad were enjoying their home in St. Clair Shores, where eighteen-year-old Riene still lived with them. Marlene and I spent as much time with them as we could; I allowed Riene to borrow my powder-blue Mercury occasionally and even host parties at our house with her friends.

While I was building up our excavating company, Riene continued to help my parents at the Light Tower. On most nights, one of them, or a couple, would staff the front desk. When my father rebuilt the place after the fire, he expanded an apartment attached to the entrance area where they could quickly spring out to greet guests. Often they would turn in late at night and sleep uninterrupted until the morning. People rarely checked in after midnight, but late-arriving guests weren't entirely uncommon.

Unfortunately, three men who came calling in the earliest hours of August 10, 1960, were the most unwelcome kinds of visitors imaginable. John Coulter, Fred Chamberlain, and Kenneth Funke may have been loitering at the Wishing Well bar on Gratiot Avenue that evening, drinking a few rounds and running low on money. The first two had long police records that included arrests for drunk and disorderly conduct, burglary, and armed robbery—but at that fateful moment, they were free. We later learned that they were part of a small criminal gang.

In any event, the three men that night were looking for quick cash, and in an era long before credit cards were common, they apparently figured a motel by the side of the road would have plenty of it. The Light Tower also provided them the convenience of being an easy in-and-out to a major highway that would help them get away, fast, before police could arrive.

Wearing masks, Coulter and Chamberlain got out of their car, went to the front door, and rang the bell. The twenty-four-year-old Coulter, at six-foot-three-inches tall, was an imposing figure and came armed with a double-barreled, sawed-off 12-gauge shotgun. Chamberlain, who at twenty-six years old was a few inches shorter, brandished a revolver.

Without looking outside at who was ringing, my father answered the door and opened it. The two, led by Chamberlain, shoved their way inside and informed him, "This is a stickup!" The expression on the face of one of them was "like he was mad, very vicious and mad," my father would recall later in court. There was $120 sitting on the front desk. Dad gave them the money, but the men said it wasn't enough and that there had to be more. My father told them there wasn't, so they started beating on him.

Then the entire situation took a much more menacing turn. Hearing the commotion, my mother, wearing her nightgown, came into the front-office area from the hallway that led to their bedroom. Coulter pointed the shotgun at her, but Dad managed to shove it aside before Chamberlain clocked him on the head. Then Chamberlain pistol-whipped my father repeatedly and knocked him onto the sofa, holding the pistol to his chest and cocking the gun.

Meanwhile, my mother bolted back through the hallway and ran out a side door so that she could get help from people who were staying in the next unit. Before Mom had a chance to pound on any doors, however, Coulter followed, coldly raised his 12-gauge, and shot her in the back, killing her. She fell into shrubs in front of unit No. 10, her blood pooling and draining the life from her body.

Riene was in her own room at the apartment and had gone to bed about 11 p.m. She was used to hearing noises around the motel after normal hours, mostly from drunks. But that night she heard a louder ruckus than usual, woke up and looked down the hall toward the office area. She saw Chamberlain and our father, and then crept away silently before either saw her. Next, Coulter went into my parents' bedroom and said to my father, simply, "I just killed your wife."

Riene slipped behind an organ in the main room by the front office and continued watching the three men in silence. At gunpoint, Dad led the killer and his accomplice into the bedroom, where he pointed to $100 in bills that were lying on a dresser. "Here, take the money and just leave," Dad said. One of them gathered up the cash, then Coulter and Chamberlain walked back out into the hallway and into the main room. Chamberlain was shocked to see my sister cowering by the organ. "Get down or I'll kill you," she remembered the robber saying, when he shoved the muzzle of the pistol against her.

Then, as suddenly as they'd come and devastated our family, the two men left via the bedroom door and dashed on foot to a car parked about a block away where Funke was waiting. Apparently running on blood lust, the trio stopped to commit another crime, with Coulter and Chamberlain entering a bar several miles away just twenty minutes later, threatening the owner and two waitresses and getting away with more than $1,400.

Not long thereafter, Diena got a call from the police and rushed to the Light Tower from her house nearby, but it was too late for her to do anything. "I remember trying to go out the side door where my mother had gone, but a policeman stopped me," she said. "I never did see her again until the funeral." She found our father sitting on the couch in the office. I had been the first to arrive at the motel. I was holding an ice bag to his head, which was still bleeding. Diena called a doctor to come and stitch him up.

———

Over the next several weeks and months, the loss of our mother weighed tremendously on all of us, but especially on Riene, who was moving into what was supposed to be the prime of her life. "Someone had just ruined her life; she and my mom were very close," Diena recalled. Riene also had to deal with the sometimes-subtle guilt that visits survivors of heinous crimes, as they wonder, *Why didn't this happen to me instead, or to me also?* There never would be clear answers why the killers hadn't killed her and, for that matter, our father.

"Sometimes you go through things and you're just in shock, but you move on because of your background and your faith in the Lord," Diena recalled. "That is what we had to do. John took charge."

In the most trying of times, everyone came together. Stunned by the loss of our mother and unable to disassociate the Light Tower from the awful circumstances of her death, Dad and Riene moved into our house. "Marlene took Riene in like her own sister and just showed so much love to her," recalled Diena. It benefited Riene that she could be pressed into service immediately, helping look after John Jr. and assisting Marlene in running the household. But she also needed distance, and by the fall of 1961, she had enrolled in Michigan State in East Lansing, Michigan, about a two-hour drive from our home.

Dad buried his wife of more than thirty-two years in late August 1960. The program from the funeral noted that she had been "a daughter of the church; a faithful wife and mother; a revered friend of hundreds; a conscientious example; and an industrious helpmate." Despite his grief, Dad stayed in the funeral parlor and greeted visitors for hours. As family members, friends, and business associates offered him their condolences, I remember him saying over and over again, "It's the Lord's will, and I am prepared to accept it." He was the rock for all of us at that time and leaned so much on his faith. I remember telling our pastor, Leslie Crane, "Whatever he has, I want."

Eventually, Dad recovered from his physical injuries, but became lost in emotional grief that couldn't be shaken. Fortunately, he didn't have much memory of the events because he had been knocked unconscious.

While dealing with our sense of profound loss, Marlene and I tried to keep our businesses growing. Diena and Gene, who was working for my company by then, moved with their four children to take over operation of the Light Tower, where she had pitched in behind the desk over the years.

Only the love that sustained and surrounded our family got us through some dark, dark months. God uplifted us during this time as well, we all believed, in part through the prayers of our friends at Lakeshore Presbyterian Church.

Diena said, "For a while I tried to put it out of my mind because I had to take over the business, and I had the children. At times I would break down, but I didn't do it where everybody was. We were a hugging family, so that's what we did when we all got together with my dad and my sister. We stayed together. And friends stepped in. That's what brings you through something like this—the love of people."

Local police dubbed the case as "one that must be solved" because of its brutal and wanton nature, reported the *Daily Monitor-Leader*, a newspaper in Mount Clemens, Michigan. Detective Sgt. Roy Hinkle of the Roseville Police Department told the *Battle Creek Enquirer* that the shooting was "one of the most brutal things I ever saw. Only the worst kind of man would come back and tell a man, 'I just killed your wife.' "

The psychological and spiritual shock of my mother's death rocked our family—and would reverberate for decades. Making matters worse, of course, was that two of the three thugs would remain at large for a long time. It took a tireless manhunt by several law-enforcement agencies, the dogged efforts of a couple of local detectives, and even a seemingly serendipitous conversation between U.S. sailors in Spain to bring them to justice.

CHAPTER 8

Delayed Justice

BY MID-1962 THE JUSTICE SYSTEM FINALLY managed to levy its judgments on the young men who murdered my 55-year-old mother so savagely almost two years earlier.

It was remarkable, of course, that the trio had been able to escape immediate capture, given that after they robbed the Light Tower, beat up my father, killed my mother, and threatened my sister, Riene, they nonchalantly stopped at another establishment, threatened more lives, and committed another burglary. But somehow, they disappeared into the night on August 10, 1960, probably thinking they'd never be discovered since they hadn't been caught already.

Roseville Detective Sergeant Roy Hinkle and Detective Harold Ernst of the Center Line State Police post spent thirteen months and traveled thousands of miles trying to solve the case. Leads poured in from a total of seventeen states stretching from Maine to California. Detectives ran down a total of 418 tips received on the killing that named 512 informants, according to the *Monitor-Leader*. They interrogated a mind-boggling total of 1,700 people, including many suspects. According to published reports, two of the men questioned agreed to submit to truth serum and another eighty were given lie detector tests.

Unfortunately, investigators didn't have any prime suspects in my mother's killing when police happened to pick up Coulter and Chamberlain within a month of the murder for outstanding warrants. Prosecutors soon convicted the pair of one of their burglaries, sending them to the state penitentiary in Jackson, Michigan. Several months later, in May 1961, Coulter escaped from the prison's farm camp near Houghton Lake, about 150 miles due north of Jackson, and remained at large; Chamberlain was left behind in jail. No one at that point—especially the perpetrators—had tied them to killing my mother.

Meanwhile, Funke, who'd brought only a juvenile criminal record to the Light Tower, was serving in the U.S. Navy. He had gotten out on an honorable discharge in 1960, at twenty-three years old, making him available for getaway driving that night in August. Two months after the killing, Funke re-enlisted, perhaps in hopes of staying as far away from Michigan as possible.

Of course, my sister Riene was the prosecution's star witness because she had seen much of the awful violence while hiding behind the organ at the Light Tower. Her recollection of what Coulter and Chamberlin looked like—even behind masks—was the absolute key to identifying the killers. Unfortunately, my father wasn't able to offer much help to investigators because he never got clear looks at them. That wasn't particularly surprising because Chamberlain was simultaneously lashing his head with the handle of his .38-caliber pistol and threatening to shoot him.

With police still not able to put together the puzzle about the suspects' identities, and Coulter out committing more crimes unbeknownst to law-enforcement authorities, Riene was subjected to one police line-up of potential suspects after another. At the trial in 1962, Riene estimated she had attended about forty line-ups in Mount Clemens, the seat of Macomb County, and in Detroit. Only seventeen days after the murder, police in Akron, Ohio, arrested three men for another killing there. According to the *Detroit Free Press*, my father told police that one of the suspects in that crime had eyes that resembled the masked man who beat him with a pistol, while my sister said another suspect looked like the man who shot our mother. Alas, police ultimately determined they weren't the suspects they were chasing.

Loose lips do more than sink ships; they also solve crimes. That's how investigators caught the big break that eventually led to the arrests of Coulter, Chamberlain, and Funke for the cold-blooded murder of our mother.

While we tried to emotionally regroup around one another and somehow piece our lives back together, there was still the matter of making sure her murderers were brought to justice.

An even bigger concern to us was that the three men were still at large, including a worry that they might come back and try to take out the only two people who'd seen them kill her: Riene and my father.

After Funke re-enlisted in the Navy, by early 1962 he'd been dispatched to an American base in Spain. One night, while on liberty from his ship in the Port of Barcelona, he went out for drinks with his buddies, and obviously had one too many. He shared the fact that he was the driver of the getaway car in this high-profile murder case in Michigan with one of his shipmates. A third sailor overheard their conversation and immediately went to his superiors in the Navy.

Navy intelligence officers questioned Funke about the crime, and they were able to extract a confession during the interrogation. He told them Chamberlain and Coulter had been the masked men who robbed my parents and killed my mother, while he waited outside in the car. He also confessed to helping them hold up the bar. Funke was transferred to Norfolk Naval Base in Virginia for more questioning, but then he went absent without leave. He eventually surrendered at Great Lakes Naval Training Base, north of Chicago. The Navy shipped him to Macomb County, where state prosecutors made a deal with him: Identify the murderers and you might avoid life in prison.

By September 1961, all three men had been charged with first-degree murder. Funke was in custody, and it was easy for investigators to find Chamberlain: He was still in the prison in Jackson. Their arrests were front-page news in the *Detroit Free Press*. Only Coulter remained at large, with investigators telling the public he didn't have any external identifying marks but was "known to use beatnik-type slang when he converses." For whatever reason, Coulter was still hiding in the Detroit area, and nearly a year after he escaped from the prison farm in central Michigan, police hauled him in and returned him to the Jackson prison to await trial.

Coulter and Chamberlain finally went on trial for murdering my mother and beating my father in early June 1962. Judge George Deneweth presided over the jury of ten women and two men. Chief Macomb prosecutor Steve Michaels sparred with Joseph Louisell, a well-known defense attorney representing Coulter, and Allen Chaflin, counsel for Chamberlain. I never understood how Coulter could afford Louisell because he was expensive and was purported to represent clients from the underworld. He was fierce.

Riene's testimony was key. Before she took the witness stand, our father testified that he couldn't absolutely identify the men because they were crouched for most of the time during the attack. Under relentless questioning from Louisell, Dad even allowed as how, after Chamberlain hit him with the gun and split his head open, he wasn't in full possession of his faculties. And when asked more than once by the defense if he remembered how he got from the front office to the bedroom during the episode, he simply couldn't explain.

So Michaels knew it was up to my sister to convict these men—and so did his courtroom opponents. After Michaels led her carefully to a positive, dramatic identification of Coulter and Chamberlain as they stood in the courtroom, Louisell focused his cross-examination on whether Riene, then twenty years old, could believe her senses—or her own story.

Could Riene absolutely, positively identify the two men for sure, given the dim light at night and the panic of the moment? Louisell told Riene that Coulter actually was in a police lineup she had observed at one point and wondered why she hadn't identified Coulter at that time. The defense attorney further suggested that police had asked her leading questions in showing her photos of the suspects. Louisell also tried to confuse both Rieni and our father about the height of the man carrying the sawed-off shotgun, suggesting that it was actually Chamberlain who'd fired the fatal shot.

With unbelievable strength and composure, Riene was able to persuade jurors with a detailed description of the murderer, even after Louisell tried to confuse her by telling her to remember out loud "everything that you told the police officers in describing" Coulter.

"Well," Riene began one of her longest and most convincing responses, "he was tall, approximately six feet or over, maybe an inch under. I am not sure. He had dark hair. Bushy sideburns. It just hung sort of naturally curly, curly stuff, that went away.

"He had bushy eyebrows, dark eyes as far as I could tell. They weren't large eyes. They were small. He had the pointed nose, very thin face. I couldn't see his mouth because of the mask. But the mask was pulled thin. It wasn't tight. And I could tell [his nose] was thin because of the bone structure."

Riene continued without pause, "His weight—he wasn't a heavy person. He was quite slim. I am no judge of weight so I couldn't give a guess. He was very lanky.

"Is that what you want?" Riene finished, turning the tables back on the surprised defense attorney. "That's what I said to the police."

Featuring a total of thirty-seven witnesses, the sensational criminal trial lasted two weeks. No testimony was more important than Riene's totally convincing narrative and refusal to concede any ground to the skilled defense attorneys. Under relentless, pointed, and heavy cross-examination, Riene countered their probes and stuck consistently to her observations. I was so proud of my sister's strength. "She was a very good witness," the *Monitor-Leader* quoted "court observers" as saying.

On June 27, 1962, the jury convicted Coulter of shooting and killing my mother, and Deneweth sentenced him to a mandatory life sentence without a chance of parole for first-degree murder. Unfortunately, after eighteen hours of deliberations, the jury couldn't reach a verdict on Chamberlain. He was tried again in

December 1962, and this time jurors convicted him of being an accomplice in her murder. Chamberlain also was sentenced to life in prison without the possibility of parole. In January 1963, Funke pleaded guilty to his role, and in February, thanks to his cooperation with the government, he was sentenced to life in prison with a chance for parole.

⟶

Over the next couple of decades, we began to heal from the tragedy that had destroyed our family and gradually forgot about the three men who killed my mother as they languished in prison. Funke was released on parole in the early 1980s, and we never heard about him again. Per their sentences, Coulter and Chamberlain would spend the next thirty-plus years behind bars in a federal prison in the Upper Peninsula of Michigan and were never supposed to enjoy freedom again.

But in the 1990s, Michigan Governor John Engler began looking at people like Chamberlain and Coulter as a way to save money for the state. To help close a $1.6-billion deficit that had developed in the Michigan budget under his watch, he began pondering the release of as many as 12,000 Michigan inmates. Engler's advisors believed the state could close a handful of prisons and lay off as many as 1,000 correctional officers for a savings of $120 million for one fiscal year alone.

Their argument was that the state was in trouble financially, and it cost $50,000 a year to take care of one prisoner. So they elected to examine all these prisoners to see how long they'd served and what kind of prisoners they were, and whether they were sick or not. The healthier they were, and the better prisoner they had been, the better chance they had of being paroled because they were no trouble. The governor wanted to get them out into society and see if they could become model citizens.

I was pretty active politically by then, so I was conscious of the debate going on inside the state capitol. It became very personal for me when Governor Engler, whom I considered a friend, called to ask how I would feel if Chamberlain and Coulter were released out of prison. In their fifties at that point, they had apparently been model prisoners and fit the state's new criteria for consideration of clemency.

Governor Engler called me at our vacation home in Colorado. He told me that the state was considering releasing Chamberlain, the triggerman, and he wanted to know if I was opposed to it. To be honest, so much time had gone by that those guys weren't really on my mind. I paused for a few seconds and told him, "They paid their price here on Earth."

After hanging up with Governor Engler, I shared the news with my younger sister. Riene was especially concerned because she was the one who'd fingered them. She was worried they might try to find her. I acknowledged her concerns, though I wasn't worried that any of us would be in any particular danger. Based in part on my Christian convictions, I prayerfully concluded that I wouldn't stand in the way of seeing my mother's murderers walk free.

To be honest, I wasn't particularly happy that my mother's murderers were being set free. But as Christians, we are taught to believe that we should forgive those who have sinned against us, even in the face of personal tragedy. Forgiveness is not a one-time action. The Bible makes it clear that for Jesus Christ to forgive us, we must forgive others. As Matthew 6:14–15 tells us, "For if you forgive other people when they sin against you, your Heavenly Father will also forgive you. But if you do not forgive others their sins, your Father will not forgive your sins."

We never heard from the three men. Sadly, my loving sister Riene died of heart failure in 2019.

The arc of a profound tragedy can stretch throughout lives, over the years and decades, and that certainly was the case with the destructive ripples of my mother's death for our family.

After several months of harboring his grief, and with more time alone on his hands than he ever anticipated, Dad eventually started coming over to the Light Tower during the days. But within a couple of years, he decided to escape his woes by moving to New Smyrna Beach, Florida, and investing in some apartments there.

The loss of our mother would afflict Riene in deep ways for the rest of her life. We tried to avoid talking about it, but she was so close to our mother that the memory of what happened to her would sometimes make her sad and angry.

Marlene and I hadn't given anything in philanthropy to that point, but a friend suggested it might help me with my grief if I did so in my mom's memory. So Marlene and I made a gift of $2,000 to St. John's Hospital, and to this day there's a plaque outside the room dedicated to her.

As for my grief: I admit I suppressed it to some extent, in part by talking about my mother's death very little. In 1961, I went back into my business and really buried myself in it, to some extent because of the tragedy and the grief that we'd all gone through. It kind of helped me to do that. And I decided to diversify the business some. Rather than continue to grow the excavating company, I thought we should build something for ourselves."

Just as the sorrowful murder of my mother changed the course of my family's history, my decision about a new direction for my business also would be fateful for the entire family—and all the way through to today.

CHAPTER 9

A New Vision

THE POST-WORLD WAR II ECONOMIC BOOM IN THIS country was a fantastic thing for the Greatest Generation, for generations of Americans to come, and eventually for billions of people around the world. But there were some major holes in economic progress in the United States as it ascended in the late 1940s and 1950s, and one of them was the inability of the nation to provide adequate housing for all the folks who were pouring into the major job centers of the era, such as metro Detroit. Many thousands of people had migrated to the Motor City to help make material for the Arsenal of Democracy and wanted to stay after the war. Then the GIs came back to Michigan, got married, began having kids, and—well, there just weren't enough decent places for everyone to live.

Trailer houses became a big part of the solution. Some historians have suggested that the first mobile homes were small cottages on the Outer Banks of North Carolina in the 1870s. As the tides of the Atlantic Ocean rose and fell, horses moved them up and down the beach to avoid flooding. Those houses weren't really mobile, however, and couldn't be transported across the country on wheels.

Mobile homes—defined here as dwellings hauled by motorized vehicles, not Conestoga wagons (the horse-drawn freight wagons with canvas coverings over arched wooden hoops that were popular in Maryland, Ohio, Pennsylvania, and Virginia from 1820 to 1840)—have been around nearly as long as automobiles. They arose early in the 20th century to enable motorists to make long trips on an American road system that remained highly underdeveloped at that point, and that still lacked convenient overnight accommodations. These platforms grew and evolved into a form of long-term housing by World War II. Then the two types of trailers would diverge permanently, into mobile homes and recreational vehicles, within another decade.

In the infancy of the automobile, American drivers sought to escape the pollution and overcrowding of big cities and escape to the fresh air of the countryside or beaches. They would take along tents and enough amenities that they could simply pull off by the side of a road, pitch the tent, awake, take it down and resume their travels the next morning. These were the beginnings of what became a cultural mainstay of American life: the vacation by car.

Soon wealthier motorists would begin having craftsmen build what they called "trailers," according to Frank Rolfe, a Texas-based mobile-home-park operator who taught a seminar, "Mobile Home University," to people in the industry. They were obviously a much cushier and safer means of staying by the side of the road, and these trailers could even be decorated with mahogany interiors, crystal chandeliers, and names on the outside, just like yachts.

The Smithsonian credits Pierce Arrow's Touring Landau as being America's first recreational vehicle in 1910. According to Crystal Adkins of *Mobile Home Living*, "The Touring Landau used a patented fifth wheel trailer hitch mechanism that permanently attached to the automobile. The model was shown at Madison Square Garden and offered to the public for $8,250. It lists a phone line to connect the trailer to the driver and had a chamber pot."

Mae West and other Hollywood royalty owned trailers, according to Rolfe, as did blueblood families including the Rockefellers, the Vanderbilts, and the Astors. The growth and celebration of trailers as "recreational" vehicles culminated in the 1954 movie *The Long, Long Trailer*, which starred Lucille Ball and Desi Arnaz as honeymooners who spend a madcap week touring America in a New Moon trailer pulled by a Mercury Monterey. Nowadays, RVs are more popular than ever, and celebrities such as the actor Matthew McConaughey, who owns several Airstreams, help stoke the mystique behind the hobby.

The original "trailer parks," Rolfe said, were free places to park trailers that cities built in order to lure wealthy travelers—and their money—to local retailers. But the term soon would take on a much more negative connotation as an outgrowth of the same dynamics that created an entirely new type of trailer beginning in the 1930s: the mobile home.

The stock market crash of 1929 and the subsequent Great Depression brought about a reevaluation of the purpose of trailers. "People are losing their homes, losing their farms, losing their jobs," as Rolfe put it in the seminar. "They need to find someplace to live that's cheap, and people realize, well, those upscale trailer things—we could live in those, couldn't we? If we're able to spend one night in them, why can't we spend 365 nights in them?"

This created another problem: so many families had trailers and needed a place to park them—and not just for one night. "That was an issue because some people weren't taught the proper manners for general decency and would litter, make a lot of noise, and leave the locals with a bad opinion of the people traveling," Adkins wrote. "It was getting out of hand and many towns were restricting trailer parks altogether because they worried about property values, crime, and a lower tax base. Some towns were cashing in and opening pay-by-night parks though they had to limit the number of nights trailers could stay. Otherwise, some trailer owners would stay for months."

World War II was the next life-changing event that provided momentum to mobile homes, as the U.S. government rather suddenly required massive amounts of base housing for all its newly recruited servicemen as well as places to accommodate the thousands of workers who were migrating to production centers to build tanks, bombers, and jeeps. With mobile home sales declining dramatically because of the war, the industry persuaded the U.S. government that trailers were the perfect solution. The military quickly scarfed up a half-million mobile dwellings and placed them around the country, which Rolfe said was about the entire capacity of an industry that only had started in earnest during the 1930s.

Many of the soldiers and their families had left stick-built homes and apartment buildings to move into trailers for the first time. They were quickly built and poorly constructed of lesser materials, as most of the good wood and metal were going to the war effort. Trailer living quickly earned a bad reputation as a result.

For instance, at the Willow Run bomber plant, which Ford Motor Company built between Ypsilanti Township and Belleville, Michigan, to produce B-24 Liberator heavy bombers, an estimated half of its 43,000 workers were living in trailers (without indoor plumbing). Even the mobile homes for families of factory workers were tightly organized like military barracks, of course, in the most convenient tracts near plants, making them efficient and low-cost—but also cookie cutter-like and not very appealing to the eye.

"Trailer park living was hard living and there were pros and cons for both the federal and private parks," Adkins wrote. "There was rarely enough water and trash receptacles were often overfilling in both types of parks. Mud was a big issue in the parks during the winter and spring too. . . . In some of the federal parks, wooded sidewalks were built to remedy the mud issue but you couldn't modify or build onto the trailers at all."

After the war ended, many of these same trailers were hauled into service as student housing to accommodate the crush of ex-soldiers taking advantage of the GI bill, Rolfe said. That explained the common sight of trailer parks near American universities and colleges as they grew. And many would stay in these trailers as they went on to post-graduate training in law, medicine, or science. Once the war was over, the trailers were built of better materials and with new amenities. They were much more desirable. "For one brief moment in American history in the 1950s," Rolfe said, "if you lived in a mobile home in a mobile-home park, you had higher demographics than those who lived in stick-build homes."

That would change in a hurry.

The 1950s was when the fledgling notion of a mobile home was permanently shaped into popular definition as an inexpensive, probably even rickety, confined space occupied by lower-class Americans who couldn't afford—or maybe didn't want—to go anywhere else. As the generation born in the first half of the century matured and began making their mark on the latter half, they built traditional homes in cities, fleshed out suburbs, and expanded small towns and rural outposts across America. They were fulfilling their demographic destiny, and for the most part they weren't going to do so living in an eight-foot-wide trailer situated on the wrong side of the railroad tracks.

Trailers that were complete enough to be considered manufactured houses began appearing in the 1950s. Soon pioneering companies would improve the formula by building a house trailer in two halves that could be transported within the government's eight-foot-wide regulation for the highway, and then be put together at a site. There were even telescoping side panels and telescoping second stories.

In 1952, trailer manufacturer Marshfield Homes began calling its units "mobile homes." The company, based in Marshfield, Wisconsin, also figured out a way around size restrictions for transporting house trailers by getting construction permits for hauling overwide units. Branded Tenwide, the ten-foot-wide Marshfield Homes model allowed space for a long corridor within the trailer, which gave designers room to make the interior more closely resemble the layout of a site-built home.

Such innovations moved the trailer home further along the path of emphasizing occupancy rather than mobility and more deeply into the mainstream of America's scramble for affordable housing. Meanwhile, trailer manufacturers pressed for improvements in trailer parks. But they couldn't compete with tract houses that became the preferred means of affordable housing and the first step toward achieving the American Dream. Offered by construction companies including Levitt & Sons, tract houses also were prefabricated, like house trailers, but were put together on-site and conveyed a sense of permanence: They couldn't be moved.

Other factors stacked up against mobile homes. "The Federal Housing Authority did not even begin insuring mortgages for trailer homes until 1971, which meant that owners faced 'hidden fees and penalties' that offset their supposedly cheap price tags," wrote Nina Renata Aron in a history of mobile homes on Timeline.com. "This also made trailer residents a target of resentment, since they weren't paying property taxes. Moreover, since desirable plots of land were used for new suburban home construction, trailer parks were often consigned to unappealing lots."

So house trailers remained largely the domain of what was considered the lowest segment of American society, and trailer parks became the places where people who weren't keeping up with the Joneses settled. They became popularly perceived as "deviant, dystopian wastelands set on the fringe of the metropolis," wrote Nancy Isenberg in her 2016 book *White Trash: The 400-Year Untold History of Class in America*.

Trailer-park occupants felt the disdain. "In the '40s and '50s, we were thought of as trailer trash," said an interviewee in the 2012 documentary *Suburbs on Wheels: A History of American Trailer Parks*. "I don't know if people didn't want anything to do with us because we lived in these little buildings, but we just stuck together, we hung together, we stuck up for each other."

The ultimate irony, of course, was that "mobile" homes became anything but mobile—once put in place in a trailer park, usually they were there for decades, only "moved" when they'd worn out their useful life. So for many occupants, trailer parks became something akin to prisons without bars.

All of this made trailer parks about the last place anyone would look for the opportunity to make a name. But then I came along with a fresh vision on how to make them more desirable.

In essence, I had my own idea of how trailer parks originated, attributing their development in large part to local governments that wanted to clean up after World War II and participate in the post-war boom. It was okay during the war if men were living in trailers, sitting on curbs in residential areas, and dumping their waste onto the streets. But after the war, communities would say, "We've got to clean up and get rid of these trailers. Here are spots where they must go." First they were called trailer camps.

Then people said they needed sanitation and water, and they became mobile-home parks or trailer parks.

These trailer parks were just places where communities deposited—and hoped to hide—the unsightliness of their cast-offs, without much regard for how those people actually had to live. But Marlene and I had seen how things could be different.

The first mobile-home park in America was established in 1955 in Bradenton, Florida, encompassing 160 acres and hundreds of people, mainly retirees, who bought individual lots for their mobile homes and paid a monthly fee for amenities. They were treated to shuffleboard courts, a grocery store, a marina, and many strategically placed palm trees. Covenants governed exterior additions to the trailers as well as a lot and its maintenance. Even within the park, there were zoning restrictions regarding where people could have children or pets.

While traveling to Florida and Arizona, we saw these kinds of properties. With my ever-churning developer's mind, I wondered, *If this kind of trailer park works down there, why couldn't it work in Michigan?*

We decided we could build a respectable community for people so they didn't have to live in trailer camps. We started with the idea of improving this way of life so people would be proud of it.

Wheels would have to be removed from the trailers and the structure put on footings that my company would pour. Every trailer would be required to have a front door and brick siding. Each trailer site would have a tree. Each household would pay a rental fee of $300 a month, and people could live a new life.

Just as important to my approach to each rental site was my vision for the entire neighborhood. My "trailer parks" would be rebranded as "five-star communities," with a grand entrance, swimming pool, putting green, and a clubhouse prominently situated close to the street outside.

We wanted to raise the image of mobile-home living and educate people about the lifestyle. We knew it wouldn't be easy with the stigma attached to what people called "trailer parks."

But once people realized that it was a community, and that within the community they had a lot of things they could do and a lot of activities and so on, we could bring it to a place where there was a sense of pride in ownership.

The Chateau name came later. My partner and I designed a neighborhood center for the first community that featured a mansard roof, a classic design that's characterized by two slopes on each side of the roof with the lower slope, containing dormer windows, at a steeper angle than the upper. It's also called a French roof. So there was a real French flavor there, and Marlene thought, "Let's call it 'Chateau Estates.' " Her thinking was that these homes each would be sort of a chateau for those families. And that was the name that stuck for our company for all those years.

Along the way, I left Lakeview Excavating and sold to the Trombley brothers in favor of putting my energy and resources into Chateau Estates. Now my new partner, Pete Ministrelli, and I were equal partners in Chateau. I would be able to leverage my excavating experience to develop the sites for Chateau communities and take care of the underground infrastructure, while Pete's specialties were paving the streets and constructing the clubhouses and other facilities.

I'll admit that we knew absolutely nothing about mobile home communities in the beginning. Probably the most we knew was that trailers were sold on the same kind of lots that used cars were sold on. But we figured that the combination of the two of us would be good for starting this business. So Pete and I met in a parking lot where I pulled out some plans for the first mobile-home community.

When this idea first came to me, there was just one problem: I had no place to establish my first community. But on a family drive one Sunday after church, I noticed a homemade sign on a tree near the intersection of Utica and Van Dyke roads in Clinton Township, just a few miles from our house in Fraser.

The sign said, "30 Acres for Sale. Zoned Trailer."

CHAPTER 10

Stretching

FOR MARLENE AND I, THE 1960S WAS A PERIOD of stretching in every way. Our household was complete, but our kids were growing and coming into their own. Our family was living in a spacious home we loved, but we were having to utilize it in new ways to support our broadening social lives. And while our marriage had created a comfortable foundation for us, each was finding ways to branch out that were significant to us as individuals as well as to the family, such as through our church.

Marlene found out that the principal of Lakeview High School needed a coach for a group of girls who hadn't made the cheer-leading squad—but nonetheless were athletically talented and wanted to start a dance team. They would perform, say, between junior varsity and varsity football games or at halftimes. With her vast experience as a professional dancer, Marlene dutifully taught them and coached them up three times a week for most of the school year.

"I kind of had a soft spot for Lakeview because John had gone there," Marlene said. "I lived quite a distance away, but I decided to do it. These weren't pom-pom girls, but girls who could dance. The school mascot was the Huskies, so we named them the Huskettes. And I did that on a volunteer basis for the next fourteen years."

Meanwhile, I was expanding my company and extending my leadership in developing metro Detroit and the mobile-home community market in various ways. Chateau Estates was just beginning to take shape. But through Lakeview Excavating, the Trombley brothers and I were becoming key figures in the suburban expansion that was convulsing southeastern Michigan in the early 1960s.

One of the hot spots for that transformation was Troy, in the southern part of Oakland County and yet far enough from Detroit that it was still mostly farm pastures in those days. Within a few decades, a mile-long corridor of upscale offices, stores, hotels, and apartment complexes along 16-Mile Road, known there as Big Beaver Road, would become the second-largest center of finan-cial heft and commercial significance in southeastern Michigan, a runner-up only to downtown Detroit itself.

But in 1964, a transcendent Troy was only a dream of pioneering developers Max and Phillip Stollman of Biltmore Properties, along with Norman Cohen and Sam Frankel, when they began construction of the Somerset Apartments along with the original Somerset Mall. In an interview with the Troy Historic Village in 2015, Cohen remembered that "cows were grazing across the street from Saks Fifth Avenue the day the store opened" in 1969. It would take three decades and heavy litigation for the completion of the Somerset Collection as a premier national luxury-shopping attraction, but the entire complex spanning Big Beaver Road finally would be open by the late 1990s.

In the beginning, I wasn't sure their dream would ever come to fruition. I remember standing with Frankel in pre-development days when he told me, "We're going to put 2,000 apartments here and then the shopping center." The only thing I saw was a lot of land covered in weeds. However, they eventually did hire us to install the utilities for all those apartments and then for Somerset.

Though I was a conservative Dutch Protestant who'd grown up mainly around people like me, I learned to work with a development community in the northwest suburbs of Detroit of people who were mostly Jewish. While I was an outsider and didn't know much about their heritage or religion, I leaned on one of my biggest strengths: building one-on-one relationships. I tried to become a part of the Jewish community as much as I could. In fact, I must have gone to a hundred fundraising dinners for a Jewish college that the Stollmans supported.

In gaining their respect—and their business—as a goy, I also relied on demonstrating complete honesty and utter dependability. At one point, Phillip Stollman began calling me his "son," even though he had three actual sons who were older than me. Each of them took me under his wing and trusted me. In fact, there were never written contracts when I worked with them. Everything we did together was secured the old-fashioned way—by a handshake.

Even without a written agreement, I knew Cohen and the Stollmans would pay me on time, and they had a bedrock expectation that I would complete jobs quickly and well. For any partnership to work, developers had to have confidence that I could deliver. Since we were installing underground utilities, we were the lead people in actually developing the property. Developers wanted to hire someone who they knew would step up and do it on time. They reached a place where they were comfortable with our company.

———

My growing reputation in the development community also paid dividends as Lakeview Excavating extended its reach by building its own strip-mall shopping centers, small apartment buildings, and other properties in Macomb County.

For instance, a developer would buy a one-hundred-acre parcel of land from a farmer and divide it with a portion for a shopping center, a portion for industrial use, and a portion for residential use. But you had to go to the community to make sure it fit into its strategic land use plan, and you had to do that before you purchased the property.

So one of my most important responsibilities was obtaining zoning approvals from city governments. The zoning officers were typically land planners and other lower-level officials who didn't make a lot of money but who had a lot of authority. My clients were depending on me to get approvals from these people. In some cases, I'd lie awake at night worrying about whether I would get certain letters of acceptance; but I always did. The end result is that I became known as a guy who could move around, not offend anyone necessarily, and get things approved—quickly and on time.

In fact, developers began competing to partner with me as they envisioned building tracts of houses in the suburbs for people leaving Detroit, whose ranks kept growing through the early 1960s (and virtually exploded after the riots in the city in 1967 and 1968). Sometimes those who came to me weren't developers at all, but leaders of flocks.

For example, a priest for a Catholic congregation in Detroit approached me and said he represented one hundred families who wanted to leave Detroit and build houses in the same neighborhood. If I would help them, the entire group was prepared to leave the city for the suburbs. Often they would want to move to Warren, and I had good relationships with the zoning officials there. Too many bad developers had harmed cities like Warren, but a group of one hundred Catholics received quite a bit of respect and attention when they appeared before the city council. If I went along with them, and the city officials knew they could trust me, it was a lot easier to get things done.

Over the decades, as I left Lakeview Excavating and focused on expanding Chateau Estates, I found that I was able to build relationships and a layer of confidence in the developer world in every part of the United States.

In our division of labor at Chateau Estates, I increasingly became Mr. Outside, dealing with potential clients and partners and the public, while Pete Ministrelli functioned as Mr. Inside, directing operations and making sure jobs were getting done.

And in that role, as I pivoted to pursue my vision of building and owning five-star mobile-home communities, I had to dig into the tool bag of every personality attribute in my possession. Patience, charm, empathy, shrewdness, wit, chattiness—each would be required in abundance for me to succeed in putting together the pieces of each development and to see them through to completion.

What I faced was endemic to the industry I was trying to help build. In the documentary *Suburbs on Wheels*, John Crean explained this common predicament for trailer-park developers who were working across the entire country. Existing local residents were afraid such facilities "would downgrade the community," said the Californian who founded Fleetwood

Enterprises, which made RVs and manufactured homes and, like me, was a pioneer in the manufactured-housing industry. "They weren't opposed to them; they just didn't want them in their own backyard."

Echoed Pete Callender, a pioneering RV dealer in Indiana, "It was next to impossible to get a good spot to locate a mobile-home park. The zoning people would put you in a commercial area where you were surrounded by railroad tracks, or factories, or whatever else."

One favorable dynamic for Chateau Estates was that it was operating at that point only in Michigan, where we got some help along the way. After facing initial resistance in trying to site mobile-home communities in some townships in Macomb County, I lobbied politicians in the state to address the situation. The Michigan Supreme Court ended up ruling that every township in the state—the typical township measures 36 square miles—must designate a site where a trailer park could be developed. Back then, nobody wanted a mobile-home park in their backyard, but we argued that it was discriminatory and prevented people from finding affordable housing, which was a sensitive social issue.

While having to comply with the new law, the farmer-dominated township boards in Macomb County still were concerned about creating fresh eyesores in rapidly developing communities. While attempting to zone something to satisfy the Supreme Court decision, they came up with a predictable solution: they'd find sites that were on landfills or along railroad tracks, the least desirable pieces of land in town.

In addition to zoning boards, we faced a lot of resistance from concerned citizens, many of whom, to be honest, weren't very educated about our plans. In one instance, Marlene ran into an acquaintance in a local grocery store who approached her with a petition to stop the zoning for the very first mobile-home community that I wanted to build. Of course, the woman was unaware of our involvement.

"Do you know what they're going to build on the Clinton River near your house?" she asked Marlene. "One of those parks."

"You mean a mobile-home park?" Marlene replied.

"Yes," the woman said.

Finding a tactful and perhaps even productive way out of the conversation, Marlene simply told her, "I don't think I'll sign. I'll just wait and see."

On the other hand, I went out of my way to make sure I could assist local authorities with whatever help they needed to address the new state requirements that my lobbying had helped create. First and foremost, we assured them that we would build a Chateau community that was a desirable place to live, which in turn would make their townships more attractive to new residents and businesses.

Still, it wasn't always easy to navigate these new opportunities. The parties involved often had conflicting interests. As word got out that Chateau was succeeding, farmers became more open to the idea of selling prime real estate to me, and thus cashing out handsomely from a lifetime investment in their land. In turn, I welcomed the possibilities for establishing communities in more desirable locations, even if it cost us more money to buy the land.

Still, planners and other officials in the growing suburban communities of Macomb County also represented the concerns of existing residents and taxpayers, who were understandably very wary of new developments that could invite riffraff right next door. We were still trying to shake the negative image of trailer parks, even if the mobile homes we were selling were much different than the ones of the past.

So on the one hand, I had to assess, sometimes deflect, and sometimes reel in farmers whose cropland I might buy for establishing a mobile-home community. I could get exhausted by some of the resulting emotional rollercoasters, and I would get Marlene involved as well. In the event of a sale, for example, one farmer's wife wanted to know what would happen to her decades-old collection of sheet music; another was an antique dealer concerned about the disposition of her treasures, including clocks and china sets that had survived for three or four generations. She ended up giving a set of china to Marlene and me; we still eat meals off that cherished gift today. In the end, my solution was to take the time to develop relationships with the farmers and their families. Sometimes it would take a year or two, but we would eventually get to the place where we were liked, and they would make a deal with us.

Depending on the township, this wooing process could prove stunningly messy and surprisingly delightful. One time, word got out in a local newspaper that I had reached a deal with a farmer, who soon moved out of his house to make way for the bulldozers. In between, someone with a semi-truck drove up and emptied out the house. They stole the doors and everything. But Chateau Estates also found ways to leverage the transition in these properties into neighborhood goodwill. We set up a "spook house" for kids in the community to visit in one of the empty barns for Halloween. Our children were excited to make scary things, and people in town appreciated our effort.

Unfortunately, winning over communities that would host a new Chateau Estates property wasn't as easy as stuffing a Frankenstein costume with hay. I had to work hard, and often very carefully, to assure them that I would present a buttoned-up appearance and be a good citizen. We would present our plans for a beautiful entrance with wrought-iron fences and the kind of landscaping that no one else would do. No more jacking up trailers, cars on cinder blocks, or fixing boats in the driveways.

In most cases, government officials and politicians were our first obstacle. I fully leveraged what I'd already learned about working with bureaucracies from previous developments by Lakeview Excavating. When I focused on specific pieces of land or offers that came to me, I talked with the local powers at first and asked them if they would entertain my plan. In the very early stages, I would ask, "Is this a good location? What do you think?"

I would get to know the supervisors and the clerks, and I would get to know them as well as you could get to know people. In most instances, they recognized that I was a nice guy and, most importantly, that I kept my word. Sometimes they gave me a little more land because of that.

Influenced by Marlene, I wasn't above using a little bit of political theater to reassure anxious politicians. For example, to build the first Chateau Estates community at 19-Mile and Utica roads in Sterling Heights—where we first saw the farmer's "Zoned Trailer" sign—I needed to sell the notion of a mobile-home community that even township officials could be proud of.

At first they said, "We've got a site by a railroad and a sanitary landfill, and that's your place." But I said, "Wait a minute—you can't build a community on that kind of thing, with trains and garbage trucks going by. I will put you on a bus and show you the kind of community we're going to build."

So I rented a bus, and the township board took a field trip with me, trekking south to Ohio where a couple of new mobile-home communities resembled the approach that we wanted to take in Michigan. After seeing how nice they were, the board ended up agreeing to let me build.

Unfortunately, getting the go-ahead from politicians typically wasn't the last obstacle; there were local residents to contend with as well. And in most cases, having the support of a township's political powers didn't ensure popular acceptance of a "trailer park" in their backyard. So not uncommonly, at township zoning meetings where I made my presentations, I would encounter raucous and sometimes fierce hostility by residents who were opposed to my plans no matter what.

Understandably, they were concerned about property values being destroyed and schools being overwhelmed, and they would say that Chateau communities wouldn't pay their fair share of property taxes. They worried we were going to crowd the roads and create floods. Again, they weren't fully up to speed on what we wanted to do, and in some cases, we were never going to change their minds—even though I was going to try as hard as I could.

I approached these situations with calmness and composure. First, I would try to make sure that the physical surroundings for the meetings didn't exacerbate tensions. Most of these township halls weren't large enough for the meetings, so I would make arrangements to use high-school gyms for the crowds that I knew could be pretty big. I wanted to make people as comfortable as possible and feel good about coming to the meetings.

I also went out of my way not to be provocative, simply showing slides and postcards that shared mobile-home living as it could be in their community, and then answering questions. I also didn't take chances on some angry, red-faced constituent flipping out of control. Fortunately, there were never any riots, although we did have the sheriff or local police accompany us. They would take care of things to make sure we were safe.

I like to think that my interpersonal, political, and business skills helped keep Chateau Estates on track in its early days. The first community opened in 1966. As the company grew, however, the demands of success would require us to ratchet our game up to much higher new levels.

CHAPTER 11

Searching for Understanding

EVERYONE IN THE BOLL FAMILY KNEW MY
tricycle story: I worried that I would wake up one
morning in the 1970s only to find that some bank,
seeking to repossess collateral, had confiscated our
kids' trikes out of the garage. I would always add to
the story that I was just kidding and that things were
never quite that precarious for Chateau Estates. But the
reality behind the tricycle tale was more complicated
than that—and not as reassuring.

I might have started my career working below ground, but I spent most of the middle portion of it performing a high-wire act. A big challenge in gaining traction with my radical new business idea was getting financiers simply to understand, much less embrace, what I wanted to do. Bankers from Main Street to Wall Street were a notoriously conservative lot—even more than they are now. And the capital needs for Chateau Estates came long before venture investors, "angels," and GoFundMe pages gave entrepreneurs plenty of alternative sources in their search for understanding, and money.

Make no mistake: I was considered a visionary in the mobile-home industry with my radical new ideas that others struggled to wrap their heads around. In imagining Chateau communities as havens for lower-income Americans who were getting very little respect in the rest of society, and then putting my money and my reputation where my vision lay, I was widely viewed by others in the business as a gambler.

I can only guess it's how the auto industry viewed Elon Musk when he introduced the Tesla, or that Steve Jobs faced the same challenges when he turned the computer world upside down. At least Americans wanted better automobiles and computers. Most people simply wanted mobile-home parks to go away—or at least for us to hide them in places where they wouldn't be seen. A half-century ago, many of the people who could have helped facilitate my vision for Chateau either couldn't grasp it, were afraid to take a chance on it, or simply dismissed it as foolishness. Through the Sixties and Seventies, this obstacle would put itself in front of me in some vexing ways. I just wouldn't let it defeat me.

⌒

The Trombley brothers and I succeeded in getting the first Chateau Estates community off the ground, though the Trombleys eventually parted ways with me and Pete Ministrelli then became my main partner in the company. I was surprised at how well things played out in the beginning. We had 530 sites, and I thought it would take three years to sell them out, but they were all taken within eighteen months. We couldn't pour the concrete fast enough. After the Sterling Heights park filled so quickly, Pete and I began developing a couple more elsewhere in the county.

Bankers are conservative people to begin with, and many of them simply couldn't get on board with our plan. We built a high-end community for manufactured housing, and the bankers didn't believe that lower-income people would move into housing that nice. Of course, Pete and I questioned the plan many times, but ultimately it proved to be very sound. For the first park, we self-financed development of the site and it nearly bankrupted our company. But then the spaces started filling up fast, and there was no turning back. We were too far down the road.

Stanford "Bud" Stoddard was one of the financiers who just didn't see what I saw. The son of the founder of Michigan National Bank was known as a banking pioneer in the mode of his father, Howard Stoddard. For instance, under Bud Stoddard, Michigan National became an early user of ATMs and issuer of credit cards. And while each was coming up in their family businesses, Bud Stoddard had been happy to approve loans for me for Lakeview Excavating to buy bulldozers, cranes, and other construction equipment.

But even the visionary Stoddard balked mightily when I approached him on behalf of Chateau Estates to risk bigger financing so the company could build more communities. Stoddard wasn't sold on my revolutionary concept of an "upscale" trailer park. Stoddard told me, "We don't lend money for trailers."

"Bud, I've stuck my neck out and tried to show a new way of living, trying to raise the standards for mobile homes," I said. "And you've got to lend me money to pay my contractors."

After Stoddard refused, I tried another tack. He knew that Michigan National Bank financed trailer parks in Grand Rapids, so he requested that the head of that local bank come to Sterling Heights to see what I was doing. That banker, too, concluded I simply had made the Chateau property too nice. In fact, he stood on the steps of this grand clubhouse that we'd built and looked around. He said, "John, I think you've built a monument to yourself." Of course, that's the last thing I wanted to hear.

Sure, I could have approached other local bankers with my request for them to stick their necks out and finance an entirely new community concept for lower-income residents of Macomb County. But I would have been starting from square one with them. And while Stoddard was standing firm, this was the banker who'd given me enough capital to expand Lakeview.

So I tried one last thing. I went back to Bud and said, "I've made all the payments on my loans for equipment. So you're going to end up with a lot of bulldozers and cranes on your front yard if you don't make me this loan for our next community."

Finally, he agreed to make me a loan for ten years, and I had to promise to find someone to buy him out of it. Of course, that's exactly what we did, and until he passed away, he would tell people the story about how John Boll threatened to put a bunch of bulldozers in his front yard.

***

While I was pushing hard to raise the money for Chateau Estates to grow, Marlene continued to help with the business in her own ways, even as she shouldered the primary responsibility for bringing up our children and the harmony of our household, spearheaded our church involvement and social life, and continued coaching the Huskettes dance team at Lakeview High School.

Gradually, Marlene gave up the clerical and bookkeeping tasks she'd had with my companies as they grew. But she maintained a significant role as an advisor to Chateau Estates in areas ranging from decorating to human relations.

For example, she helped decorate a couple of mobile homes when owners put them up for sale because some of them were sparsely decorated and the furniture was just short of a nice showplace. As soon as they were decorated and looked like a home, they'd sell.

Marlene's other role was crucial as the company figured out not just what it meant to build a different kind of mobile-home park but also how to make it a truly worthy community of like-minded neighbors rather than just a collection of nice amenities.

So Marlene worked with the local YMCA, which already had been teaching classes at our backyard pool on Millar Road, to instruct youngsters how to swim in the Chateau pools. She hired young women to teach aerobics and exercise classes to female residents and she hired activity directors to organize bridge clubs for women and card clubs and pool leagues for men.

In addition, we developed programs that encouraged people to use the clubhouse and get to know their neighbors; otherwise, it was just a big building sitting there doing nothing. Marlene was in charge of guiding what we thought should go into that community. The goal was to create true community life.

Becoming an industry leader brought its trials—and its obligations.

At one point, for example, Chateau and other park operators came into the sights of Frank Kelley, Michigan's activist attorney general. Self-described as "the people's lawyer," Kelley achieved folk-hero status with many in Michigan during his 37-year career during both Democrat and Republican administrations as an anti-business agitator. Kelley took office in 1961 as my development activities were accelerating and he finally ended office in 1999.

At one point, Kelley decided that it was exploitative for mobile-home parks to charge initiation fees because tenants were essentially stuck in place once they'd placed their trailer within a particular community. Chateau's "entry fee" was $300.

Unlike the traditional landlord-tenant relationship, manufactured home communities are "unique because the tenant generally owns the mobile home and leases the lot upon which the mobile home is placed," Kelley wrote. Yet the "former mobility" of trailer owners "has been largely lost once the structure is transported from the factory to its site in the mobile home park."

But Chateau Estates pushed back hard against Kelley's attempt to rewrite the economics of the industry we were building. We saw it as $300 to start an entirely new way of life, and the entry fee was entirely justified because of the huge investments my company made in community infrastructure that allowed Chateau Estates to offer this new way of life. Kelley eventually backed off.

Along the way, the growth and success of Chateau Estates also caught the attention of William Milliken, a Republican who was governor of Michigan from 1969 through 1983. As mobile-home purchases increased in the state, Milliken became concerned about unprincipled operators who would make "shady deals" and take advantage of people. It was time to clean up the industry, according to Milliken. The state government had no control over these communities, and he wanted a commission to create standards, so mobile homes weren't handled like used cars. Milliken wanted me to be involved.

So I accepted Milliken's appointment to head a state body to create standard and accepted practices for the industry. It ended up being a great thing; we were in the forefront as a state, and we took on that responsibility. Eventually, in 1987, the state legislature passed the Mobile Home Commission Act, a pioneering effort that later was recognized as such by the National Association of Manufactured Homes. The law

SEARCHING FOR UNDERSTANDING   107

established rules for water supply, sewage disposal, drainage, garbage collection, insect and rodent control, and maintenance and safety. Because the standardization push increased certain costs for mobile-home manufacturers and park operators, some people in the industry weren't happy with it. But it was the right thing to do.

Even as Chateau Estates continued to grow and add communities around Michigan through the 1970s, securing capital to keep growing the business remained difficult. Another major Michigan bank, Manufacturers, created an entire mobile-home financing division so I would use that fact to educate other banking people that this wasn't such a foreign thing to get into. But banks just wouldn't make that segment grow overall as fast as our company was growing, in terms of our financial needs.

Fortunately, Ken Seaton was another banker, like Bud Stoddard, who looked past the conventional misgivings about financing "trailer parks" and saw that anything I stood behind was going to be a good investment in the end.

Seaton appreciated my professionalism and also recognized that we hired very good people to manage our developments and sales. And if you were going to lend to a trailer-park developer, the banker figured, Chateau was dealing with people with higher income to start with, an indication that they might be more inclined to keep their jobs and be able to continue paying rent to our company.

Unlike many other bankers, Seaton recognized that our company's success and essentially the collateral for any loan also were integrated into our business model. Seaton liked that we were developing communities that were adjacent or close to neighborhoods of single-family homes. Chateau properties were very compatible with these developments because of our high standards. Mobile homes in our communities weren't, in fact, very mobile. We actually took the wheels off and put the homes on a foundation. We had permanent renters. If someone decided to move or couldn't afford to stay, we could sell the unit to someone else. We rarely had a space that wasn't producing monthly rent.

Unfortunately, by the 1980s, times were difficult for all homebuilders. Hyperinflation, interest rates soaring to close to 20 percent, high unemployment, a global oil crisis, and widespread failures in the savings-and-loan industry that provided so much of the financing for American homebuyers and renters were the result of back-to-back recessions within three years from 1980 to 1982. By that point, Chateau Estates had developed and owned several communities around Michigan and even in Florida. Some builders went out of business altogether, while others needed accommodations from the banks to survive the recession.

We were fortunate to come out strong on the other side. I still chafed at how I had to keep going to bankers, hat in hand, to keep the expansion of my company going. It was like reinventing the wheel many times over to find financiers who would take the time to understand and appreciate Chateau's obviously successful business model. So I began working on a way to take the Chateau proposition to the ultimate investor: the American public.

CHAPTER 12

MY FRIENDS AND COLLEAGUES HAVE OFTEN told me that I ran Chateau Estates like an extension of my personality. I demanded diligence, rewarded creative thinking, and expected honesty. I also liked setting and meeting goals. And one of my ultimate goals—from early on, yet something I didn't share with many people—was to take my company public someday.

But before I could lead Chateau to that particular promised land, I had to build the company with determination and steadiness, site by site and community by community. And in doing so, I operated by a handful of ironclad principles.

One of them was the importance of integrity. That was demonstrated by how I lived and moved, not just what I said. I'd hope that my integrity was obvious to others in the way I conducted myself in and outside the business. I tried to be organic and authentic in everything I did, so I believe my integrity quite naturally helped me build the company.

A second bedrock principle for me was executing what today would be called "servant leadership." For me, this was simply a matter of leading people by demonstrating love for them that was motivated to a great degree by my Christian faith. Throughout life, and particularly in business, I have tried to be a leader who made God's name known. I tried to lead with humility, integrity, empathy, and flexibility. As Jesus said about leadership in Matthew 20:25-28:

"But Jesus called them together and said, 'You know that the rulers in this world lord it over their people, and officials flaunt their authority over those under them. But among you it will be different. Whoever wants to be a leader among you must be your servant, and whoever wants to be first among you must become your slave. For even the Son of Man came not to be served but to serve others and to give his life as a ransom for many.' "

I tried to respect and love people in my care. I didn't expect anyone who worked for me to do things, or do things in a way, that I wouldn't do. And I generally understood what each task and responsibility demanded from an employee because, after all, I had worked my way up through Chateau literally from below the ground. I didn't ask someone to do what I wouldn't have wanted to do, whether it was picking up garbage or cleaning our equipment. I wanted to lead by example.

A third principle, and perhaps the most important one in growing the company, was that the interests of Chateau community residents were paramount. I ensured everyone understood this idea with my own attention to details that helped define this new standard of living for the people who lived in our manufactured-home properties. We had management teams who went out and checked and did inspections. Each park had a manager who was responsible to division offices. They had to be tactful but also clearly explain our expectations for maintaining homes and communities. Before the residents moved in, they knew exactly what was expected of them.

Especially in the early years of Chateau, I was personally involved in critiquing the physical appearances of each community so they would maintain their important five-star standard. Our family spent many Sunday afternoons taking detours after church to Chateau communities in Macomb County, where Marlene would brandish a yellow legal pad and everyone would point out little things that needed to be fixed or at least checked.

Once a year, C. G. "Jeff" Kellogg, our company president, and I would go out and do what we called "white glove inspections." Jeff joined Chateau in 1973 as a project engineer and eventually rose up the ranks of our company. We would go through a list such as the condition of the flowers around the clubhouse, how clean the bathrooms were, and the appliances. We also would talk to the residents to see if things were going well, although we didn't tell them exactly why we were there. It really was a white glove type of thing, and the managers' bonuses were based partly on it. We wanted everyone to be involved in the upkeep of the community, and for the employees to have a financial stake in it, so people would have enormous pride in where they lived and worked.

Of course, how the homeowners were keeping up their homes was a potentially sensitive concern because the residents, and not Chateau, owned the homes. But if a home needed to be painted, we marked it down, and community management would address it with the homeowner. We had to help many people keep up their properties because it would have been so easy for them to slip up and fall right back into the same old trap. For instance, we required that they had to cut their grass once a week, trim and edge their lawns, and they couldn't leave weeds around their houses.

Another important principle for me was delegating as much authority as I could. I provided my employees with plenty of freedom to pursue ideas even if that meant challenging me. Some of the ideas were more ambitious than others, including some of my own. One time, I suggested we offer free rent to everyone for a year to get people to move into a community. Fortunately, Jeff pointed out that we already had people living there who were paying rent every month. As much as I could, I tried never to let my ego get in the way of making sound business decisions. If someone second-guessed what I wanted to do, I listened to those concerns. And I was humble enough to know that I couldn't keep doing everything as the company grew. I tried to hire the right people who could do the job just as well and trusted them to do it.

Through it all, another of my fundamental principles was to maintain a sense of humor around the company no matter what. I wanted people to enjoy working at Chateau. I led the way, often with pranks and practical jokes. Once after I came back from a trip, I asked Pam Davis, who was working as Jeff's assistant, to sit down across from me in my office. She quickly noticed that I was wearing a gold earring. Immediately, she thought, "Oh my God—he's lost it." I didn't say anything. Finally, I asked her if she noticed anything different about my appearance, and she replied that she couldn't believe Marlene let me get an earring. I started laughing and pulled it off—it was magnetic.

Another time, knowing quite well that Pam was an arachnophobe, I was in the Chateau offices talking with Jeff in the hall. Pam walked by us, and I asked her to take something from my hand. She figured it would just be a crumpled-up piece of paper. Instead, I dropped a live spider in her hand. Jeff and I laughed hysterically, as she quickly dropped the spider and killed it.

But even with my good humor, our struggle to raise capital wasn't a laughing matter. The company went through some difficult times economically, which forced me to regroup and regroup again. I realized if we were going to continue to grow, we had to find another source of financing.

Manufactured-home communities grew dramatically in the 1970s, with half of new housing starts in 1972 being such sites according to a history of Chateau by FundingUniverse. But the industry had overbuilt, and the properties didn't begin to fill until the mid-1980s. Then the recession of the early 1980s brought sky-high interest rates and rampant failures of savings-and-loan institutions, which were our main source of financing. Despite these challenges, we somehow continued to grow, with twenty communities in Michigan and Florida by the early 1990s.

Fortunately by then, there were social and political factors in play that were quite favorable to us. For one thing, there was a clear push at all levels of government—much like today—to produce more low-income housing. There simply weren't enough economical homes for Americans to live, and manufactured homes rebounded as a new form of affordable housing.

By then, banks were more willing to finance the development of mobile home communities because of their stability. As FundingUniverse noted, "The cost of relocating a mobile/manufactured home resulted in low resident turnover, while the low cost of operations and the low rate of loan defaults made the industry a fairly low-risk investment."

Third, Chateau had achieved a remarkable degree of differentiation from most of the rest of the industry. Frankly, our mobile home communities were better places to live. After all, Chateau had led the development of what FundingUniverse pointed out were "more pleasant surroundings" for manufactured homes, "with amenities, graceful landscaping, and the look of permanent homes" that "transformed manufactured-home communities into a desirable housing alternative."

Finally, Chateau would be able to take advantage of a corporate structure that I had been eyeing for a while: the real estate investment trust, or "REIT." President Dwight Eisenhower signed legislation in 1960 that created REITs, a new approach to income-producing real estate investments in which the best attributes of real estate and of stock-based investment were combined. Even better: Operating as a trust allowed tax-free revenues as long as the company distributed at least 95 percent of its net income to shareholders.

Shopping center developers were among the first to use the structure, then REITs spread like wildfire over the decades to applications such as railroad real estate in 1967, racetracks in 1980, and suburban office buildings and parks in the mid-1980s.

Now it was time for us to test the REIT concept that, by the early 1990s, was being applied to companies that ran manufactured-housing communities. We were doing well, but I felt I had to have more money to expand. I felt there was a real market and I wanted to take advantage of that opportunity.

Ironically, the person who had paved the way with the industry's first REITs was Sam Zell, who would end up being my future nemesis. Soon I would show the man known as the "The Grave Dancer" that he wasn't the only one who could take a collection of manufactured-home communities to Wall Street.

By this time, we had developed a mutual attraction with Merrill Lynch. Chateau Estates represented the crème de la crème of "five-star" mobile-home communities, while Merrill Lynch was the reigning expert in creating REITs and taking them public. The blue-chip investment bank was one of the ancient stalwarts of Wall Street with a bull as its mascot.

Now, you might be asking yourself, *Why would any of their clients want to invest in mobile home parks?* Because when our customers moved into one of our communities, they typically stayed about seven years. While there's not enormous year-over-year revenue growth, investors could still count on growth each year of about 1 percent above the inflation percentage. Plus, an investor would get a dividend of 7 percent each year, which is steady income.

Still, it was an uneasy courtship for a while. At first, Merrill Lynch representatives simply weren't interested. Then I insisted their bankers come out to the Midwest to see some of Chateau's communities for themselves. Finally, the Wall Streeters were persuaded to get on board.

But before my team and I could form a REIT and launch an "initial public offering," or IPO, Merrill Lynch told us that we had work to do. First and foremost, the advisors insisted the company needed to be bigger, and to be more diversified regionally, before it could become a prime candidate for its own stock offering and a place on the New York Stock Exchange. By 1992, Chateau was about a $90-million-a-year operation. But as profitable as the company was, the experts at Merrill Lynch believed Chateau needed to become at least a $100-million enterprise for IPO-marketing purposes.

I left Manhattan determined to overcome that last, huge obstacle. Taking account of our own growth, I figured we had to acquire about another $15 million in properties. I knew it wouldn't be easy, because we had to find other companies that operated at our standards. So upon returning to Michigan, I began blitzing the owners of similar communities with phone calls, probing to see if they would like to join Chateau and become part of a REIT.

It was no small matter to get the heads of other mobile-home community companies—typically, they were accomplished entrepreneurs and our competitors—to give up control of their enterprises even if they were looking for a financial exit strategy. I had to persuade these accomplished businessmen to take a back seat and allow me to take the lead in this venture, which wasn't easy.

Ned Allen was one potential partner I was determined to woo. Allen co-owned Intercoastal Communities Inc., with seventeen mobile home parks in retiree areas in Florida. In addition to the millions of dollars in additional revenues that would help get Chateau Estates over the top of that magical $100-million mark, his company offered the diversification of a Florida base. Most residents of his parks were 55 years old and older, living on fixed incomes such as pension plans. The residents didn't have particularly high incomes, but their monthly checks could be counted on. As a result, Intercoastal's communities looked a lot like ours in terms of amenities and appearance.

Within six months, I was back in Merrill Lynch's offices on Wall Street. Like Jerry Lewis revealing the amazing new overnight total in contributions for the Muscular Dystrophy telethon, I proudly told my investment bankers that Chateau Estates had acquired six new partners, including Allen's company, and a new annual run rate of $114 million. With a total of 15,261 home sites at thirty-three properties, we were among the largest mobile home park operators in the country—and our plan was to get even bigger and better.

A key exercise before a public stock offering is known as the "road show," in which company representatives and their bankers meet with investment outfits, including their brokers and salespeople, to sell them on the merits of the stock and answer their questions. Obviously, it wouldn't be easy selling potential investors in a trailer-community giant. We started off with having to prepare a storybook and the storybook had to tell the history of the company—and had to tell it well.

For Chateau's road show, Merrill Lynch fielded three teams, with Jeff and I leading one team each. Demonstrating the company's leadership and dependability were crucial to persuading these key decision-makers. So was being able to project and explain what we thought we could deliver to them, in a persuasive yet honest way.

In early 1993, Chateau's teams hit the road with Merrill Lynch and Bear Stearns, the other underwriter. We bounced around the major financial centers of the United States and Europe for a few months. Merrill Lynch talked to us often about "underpromising and overperforming," which played particularly well to my core beliefs. The smooth part of each presentation would be focusing on the obvious strengths of Chateau.

Of course, showmanship was crucial as with any sales exercise. We brought along a film of a teacher who lived in a Chateau community in Ohio who was so proud of where she lived that she took her elementary-school class on a field trip to visit it. She didn't want to tell the kids where she lived. She wanted to show them because she was proud of it.

Obviously, we never knew the kind of questions we would be asked by investor reps after we completed our sales pitch. For example, one common critique of Chateau held that we weren't aggressive enough with our rent increases. Jeff remembered, "Some of the institutional investors thought we could grow faster and be more profitable if we boosted rents more. But we didn't agree with that. We wanted customers to stay with us, and one way to do that was to be fair with rent increases, which were pretty much in line with the inflation rate." Jeff pointed out to the investors that the average renter stayed with us for seven years, which meant we were taking good care of them. We rarely had vacant home sites, which was another promising sign.

Overall, the road show went incredibly well for us. Each night after a presentation, I would call Merrill Lynch to get an update on how potential clients were responding through making commitments to buy blocks of the IPO stock to sell to their own clients. The trend was clear: There was enough of an appetite for Chateau stock that an IPO could garner an amount many times the "book value" of the company, meaning the total value of its assets.

This strengthened my hand tremendously in pushing Merrill Lynch for a higher offering price. Initially the bankers had suggested a price of just $10 to $12 a share to ensure a sellout; the last thing they wanted was to be stuck with a bunch of unwanted shares. But emboldened by the obvious enthusiasm for Chateau's IPO, I pushed back, demanding $22 a share. I told the bankers, "I told you there was a real market for this."

Our negotiations lasted until the early morning of November 16, 1993, the day we took our company public. At 2 a.m., we finally agreed on a number. Seven hours later, Marlene and I rang the bell to open the New York Stock Exchange. Within an hour and a half, the shares were completely sold out.

Indeed, investors eagerly bought up 5.7 million shares of stock in Chateau Properties, at $20 a share, meaning the stock went out at a whopping ten times its book value. The IPO raised $110 million, and we finally had the access to capital that we had been craving for further growth.

I'm proud to say that Chateau's rocket-launch performance even helped propel the entire stock market that day. In the wake of the Chateau IPO sellout, the Dow Jones Industrial average rose by about 200 points. After the closing bell, the New York Stock Exchange folks joked to me, "Can you come back tomorrow?"

But while Wall Street was more than willing to jump on our bandwagon, the ride had just begun. I had to reorganize the company, and I had to report to people, unlike before. The New York analysts would now tell me how much money I was going to make or needed to make. We had to go out and do anything we could to meet those projections.

We expanded rapidly as I had hoped. In January 1994, for instance, the company acquired a 129-site community in Spring Lake Township, Michigan, and just six months later bought Lake in the Hills, a 238-site community in Auburn Hills, Michigan.

Chateau continued to improve the quality of its communities and home sites as well as the quantity. Even after going public, I wanted to make sure that Chateau residents were happy residents, even as their expectations for a manufactured-home neighborhood continue to rise.

So for example, we began a $1-million expansion of our premier community, Chateau of Grand Blanc, in a suburban setting between metro Detroit and the industrial city of Flint. At that point, my son, John Jr., was working for me and oversaw construction of the Grand Blanc property. The amenities there not only included the customary Chateau clubhouse and swimming pool, but also a baseball diamond, volleyball and basketball courts, two playgrounds, a games room, and a fitness center. The Grand Blanc community also added seventy-eight sites for multisection homes on lots of up to 6,000 square feet, largest in the company.

———

True to our fun-loving sides, Marlene and I were able to enjoy the once-in-a-lifetime opportunity offered by the IPO in the most exciting city in America. It wasn't just ringing the bell at the Exchange but also taking in all the sights with an exhilaration we'd never been able to experience on previous trips to the

Big Apple. We not only kept pinching ourselves but also continually thanking God for the blessings He'd brought to our lives.

For Marlene and I, the excitement of the moment in New York was one thing. But it was nothing next to the anticipation of getting back to Michigan and sharing our new good fortune with our family, friends, and employees.

CHAPTER 13
The Grave Dancer

SAM ZELL HAD MONEY, HE HAD MOXIE, AND HE had a long track record of getting his way buying real estate and companies that didn't necessarily want to be bought. In 1997, this real-life Gordon Gekko had his sights set on acquiring the company I and others had poured blood, sweat, and tears into for more than three decades.

By then, Chateau Properties had grown to a collection of forty-seven communities in five states, including twenty-five in Michigan, with more than 200,000 home sites. Once we took the company public in 1993, Chateau Properties was rewarding investors by disbursing dividends at the sixth-highest growth rate of any public company in Michigan according to an analysis by TopBiz Network Inc. in 1996, and its revenue growth of 29 percent in 1995 placed it at #20 in the *Crain's* Detroit Business list of fastest-expanding Michigan companies. The *Detroit Free Press* called Chateau Properties "one of the best companies in the business" and *The New York Times* declared it "the premier operator of mobile-home parks in the country."

Yet we wanted to make our company even bigger, more profitable, and more attractive to investors and give it a stronger credit profile, resulting in lower financing costs.

So in mid-1996, we negotiated a $287-million merger with ROC Communities, a manufactured-housing developer that was based in Englewood, Colorado. It was a merger of equals— neither ROC nor Chateau would buy the other out. I would be chairman of the new company's board while Gary McDaniel, who was chairman of ROC, would become chief executive officer. ROC would contribute the new chief operating officer, while our president, Jeff Kellogg, would be its president and Chateau's Tamara Fischer, who ultimately would marry Kellogg, would become the new company's chief financial officer.

The companies were about the same size, with Chateau's revenues for 1995 coming in at about $62 million and ROC's at $51.5 million. The new company would have a combined 160 owned or managed properties containing nearly 50,000 home sites in thirty states, with combined annual revenues of about $125 million. Our new company would become the industry's largest player; Zell's Manufactured Home Communities' revenues were about $105 million a year.

Clearly, Zell wasn't going to relinquish his title of mobile home king without a fight.

A few weeks after we announced the proposed merger with ROC on July 18, 1996, Zell telephoned me on a Friday afternoon, as I was getting ready to travel up north for a couple of weeks of boating with my family.

"John, I'd like to meet with you," Zell told me.

"Mr. Zell, I have no problem meeting with you, but I just happen to be leaving on vacation and won't be back for a couple of weeks," I replied.

"Mr. Boll, in a couple of weeks you won't own Chateau," Zell warned me.

Zell and I couldn't have been more different. He was a Chicago-based billionaire financier who called himself "The Grave Dancer," a self-described financial vulture who succeeded in part through manipulation and intimidation. He had a reputation of bottom feeding on distressed real estate properties and bringing struggling companies back from the dead.

"Some might see buying and creating value from others' mistakes as a form of exploitation, but I see it as giving neglected or devalued assets, in any industry, new life," Zell wrote in his 2017 book *Am I Being Too Subtle?* "And often in my career I've been the only bidder for them—the last chance for a resurrection. I'm not claiming to be altruistic—just optimistic, and confident that I can turn those assets around."

At various times, Zell's affiliates have owned Schwinn Bicycle Company, the mattress company Sealy, media giant Tribune Company, and the department store chain Broadway Stores. While I might have questioned his ethics and modus operandi, it was difficult to ignore his track record.

Zell's family had fled Poland just before the Nazi occupation and moved to the Chicago suburbs, where his father became a wholesale jeweler and invested in real estate. Zell graduated from the University of Michigan and then went on to law school there. During his college days, he began managing student apartments for a variety of landlords, with the portfolio under his supervision eventually growing from fifteen units to 4,000—including more than one hundred units that he purchased personally. Although he graduated and enlisted at a blue-chip firm in Chicago with every intention of making a career there, it was clear quickly that the corporate law wouldn't satisfy him.

Instead, Zell went about building one of the most remarkable careers ever compiled in real-estate finance and corporate activism. Zell's ambition, aggressiveness, and quick mind allowed him to exploit inefficiencies and others' missed opportunities in commercial and residential properties. Through the aftermath of the 1980s real-estate collapse and the 1990s, Zell built his firm, Equity Group Investments, on what he later called the "incredible inefficiency" of real-estate investment at the time.

Over time while becoming a billionaire, Zell also proved skillful at exploiting weaknesses and finding opportunities in corporate equities, which contributed to the Grave Dancer nickname he embraced. For instance, he had helped take Revco, the drugstore chain, out of bankruptcy, so he owned a 20 percent stake. Then in early 1997, CVS paid $3.87 billion to consolidate with Revco into an even bigger drugstore chain, and Zell mopped up. Of course, the part of Zell's empire that concerned me was Manufactured Home Communities.

We met at the City Airport in Detroit. Immediately, I figured out how different we were—and I wasn't the only one who noticed. "He flies in and is extremely foul-mouthed and crass," said Fischer, who was at the meeting with me. "And Zell was super arrogant, the complete opposite of John."

Zell didn't wait long to tell me what he was going to do. Despite our previously announced deal with ROC, he told me that he was going to acquire my company, with or without my cooperation.

In August 1996, Manufactured Home made public its proposal for a simple takeover of Chateau. Zell held a press conference where he very effectively played the game of public pressuring that he knew so well. Zell's company would pay Chateau shareholders $387 million, or $26 a share, a 17 percent premium over the stock's closing price the day before the ROC transaction was announced. His offer would provide Chateau shareholders with "substantially greater value and benefits than the proposed transaction" with ROC, Zell said in a press release.

In a letter to Chateau formally proposing his deal, Zell made his point loud and clear: "We are determined to take every appropriate action to successfully consummate this transaction."

A few days later, another one of our rivals, REIT Sun Communities of Farmington Hills, Michigan, made an unsolicited offer of $380 million to acquire my company. Suddenly my company was being attacked from all sides.

I was well aware of Zell's reputation and business acumen even before his attempt at a hostile takeover of my company. Before the initial public offering of stock for Chateau Properties in 1993, one of our advisors from the Merrill Lynch investment bank suggested that we not take the company public and simply sell it to Zell. I wasn't interested. It was my dream to take our company to Wall Street, and I certainly wasn't going to turn over what I had built to someone like him.

First and foremost, there were two important groups I wanted to protect from Zell. The first group was the many residents of Chateau communities, who would have suffered if the properties weren't managed with the same standard we established in the very beginning.

And there was another group of people who absolutely deserved my protection in the face of Zell's hostility: the partners who had helped me build the company over the years, especially the other owners of self-developed mobile-home communities who pitched in with Chateau Properties and sold out in exchange for a stake in our growing company rather than for cash.

When Chateau went public, these operators, who often stayed on to manage the communities, became partners in the future success of Chateau Properties through special shares of ownership, "Operating Partnership Units." About 60 percent of the equity in Chateau was held in OPUs. Those non-voting partners had a low-cost basis for their holdings and would have faced huge tax liabilities if they sold for cash.

It was protecting the interests of those residents, business partners, long-time employees, and other associates who had remained loyal to Chateau for so many years that became the driving force behind my determination to keep Chateau Properties out of Zell's hands.

"That's where I saw some of the strength of John than I hadn't seen before," said Rich Levin, who was an outside attorney for Chateau on the way to becoming a key player in our merger defense. "He had to lead the company through a very precarious time, because Sam Zell is smart and aggressive, and he wanted to own Chateau. He put a proposal on the table that in many respects was extremely brilliant, because it drove a bit of a wedge between the historical people who formed the company and the public shareholders. So it became very challenging."

Understanding that Chateau's OPU holders had little incentive to sell out, Zell tried to take advantage by stiff-arming them and focusing instead on getting regular shareholders to sell to him. So he offered holders of Chateau common stock $26 a share in cash and preferred stock holders the equivalent of just $21 a share. Analysts said it was an attempt to get stockholders to pressure company officers to close the deal.

"The offer that Sam made was unfair to about 60 percent of our ownership," Fischer said. Or as Kellogg put it, Zell "thought the only people who would vote on his offer would be shareholders, and they aren't loyal to companies but to their investments, as they should be. That was his play."

Of course, I firmly believed that the best for everyone involved in Chateau—directors, partners, shareholders, OPU holders, employees, and Marlene and our family—would be to stay the course and complete the company's proposed merger with ROC. Fortunately, I wasn't alone. "We had outside advisors who'd been through this sort of thing a million times, and it was their thorough analysis and evaluation that the best course of action for everyone was to move forward with our merger," Fischer said. "They and our board believed that we could deliver the best outcome for shareholders over the long run, and that selling out to Zell wasn't the best path."

No matter. The drama around the future of Chateau heightened for months in late 1996, with Manufactured Home and Sun Properties sweetening their offers, and Zell launching a hostile takeover bid and unsuccessfully trying to get a judge to issue a restraining order against completion of the Chateau-ROC merger. Meanwhile, David Helfand, president of Manufactured Home Communities, was "going around trying to set up meetings with our [OPU] holders about all the things they said we weren't doing right," Fischer said.

I'm not going to lie: It was a very difficult time for me. All of a sudden, an outsider was trying to take away something that I had spent a lifetime building. I was in danger of losing control of my company through a technical restructuring that was on the table. It was a tremendously stressful time because it could have gone one way or the other. Regardless, I wanted to find a solution and expressed confidence to my management team, "We're going to get this done. Let's find how to do this. There must be a way."

Meanwhile, Zell continued to curry support in the court of public opinion, an arena where he excelled. One of his devices was an annual New Year's message that he sent to journalists as well as investors, business partners, and friends. It came in the form of tiny singing, dancing, battery-powered kinetic figurines that would entertainingly expound on some aspect of Zell's business philosophy.

In 1996, for instance, Zell's holiday statue attacked corporate bloat. But as the calendar flipped to 1997 without a resolution to his struggle with me, Zell had a new target for his New Year's Day missive. The figures in his latest figurine crooned original lyrics penned by Zell, a song called "Let's Consolidate," to the tune of Cole Porter's "Let's Do It." According to Doron Levin, a recipient who then was a columnist for the *Detroit Free Press*, the song went like this:

MCIs do it, GM guys do it / *Even airlines on the fly do it* /*Let's do it* / *Let's consolidate!* He even took a jab at me in a later verse: *Some who refuse to do it* / *Sell their shareholders a crock* / *You'll recall a few were screwed pursuant to it* / *Between a Chateau and a roc(k)*.

Fortunately, in the end, none of this could save Zell's bid. It finally floundered beneath an unexpected trump card by Chateau—an ironic bit of just deserts for a man who so often used some kind of surprise twist to subdue his targets. While searching for a way to solidify our deal against Zell's relentless attacks, about a dozen attorneys and accountants for Chateau and ROC were meeting in a conference room in New York in early 1997 when one of them came up with a brilliant idea: remove the incentive for OPU holders to go with Zell by proposing to convert the units to common shares of stock.

"We were all sitting around when [this attorney] said, 'What happens if we essentially reverse the merger process, not merging this way, but that way?' " Kellogg said. "Everyone's eyes popped open. It was clearly a huge relief for us."

Chateau and ROC asked the Internal Revenue Service for a private ruling on whether they could execute the exchange for stock with willing OPU holders and yet protect them from the potential tax consequences. "This was a structure that never had been tried before in the REIT industry," Levin said, "and yet it

My childhood days

My sister, Diena, and me

My grandfather, Anton Boll, with his family's
shipping company in the Netherlands

Marlene as a young dancer

1927 – My dad and mom

1934 – Traveling back to
the Netherlands with
my mom and sister

1934 – Me with my mother,
Abeldiena, and sister, Diena,
in the Netherlands

My Army days

1951 – Marlene and I
in South Carolina

My family – me with my
dad, mom, and sisters

1951 – *South Macomb News ... my parents Lighthouse Restaurant burns with thousands of dollars in damages*

1953 – Marlene Miller, twenty years old

Marlene (second from the right) dancing with the Rockettes

Marlene with the Roxyettes

1953 – Fun at the beach
while dating

1954 – Anton and Abeldiena
Boll at the Light Tower Motel

Our wedding day – June 19, 1954

Marlene on our wedding day with her dear mother

1955 – Moving into our first home in Roseville, Michigan

My powder-blue Mercury

My dad and I enjoying time together on the water

Chateau Estates —
a five-star community . . .
we had only just begun

1959 – My dear mother, Abeldiena Boll

Grandma Boll and John Jr.

1960 – The flood on Millar Road

1961 – *The Daily Monitor Leader . . . the unbelievable tragedy
of the loss of my mother was in newspapers often*

1964 – In Florida with John Jr. and Lora

John Jr., Lora, Marlene, and me

1966 – Millar Road with our family

1968 – Our family

1969 – First time skiing at Boyne, Michigan

Sugar Loaf skiing

Summer boat trips

Lina Miller – Marlene's mom's 80th birthday

1982 – Grosse Pointe Yacht Club

Our gift to the Grosse Pointe Yacht Club – *The Mariner*

1986 – Family trip to Europe

With our dear friend Lot

1990 – Climbing a 14er in Colorado

1990 – Racing in Beaver Creek, Colorado

On this day
December 3, 1999

John A. Boll

Chairman of the Board of Chateau Communities, Inc.
Rang the closing bell at the New York Stock Exchange

NYSE
THE NEW YORK STOCK EXCHANGE
The world puts its stock in us.®

William R. Johnston
President

1993 – NYSE Ringing the Bell Certificate

1993 – NYSE Ringing the Bell

1994 – Colorado anniversary party — "Trust Me"

President and Mrs. Ford, Marlene, and me

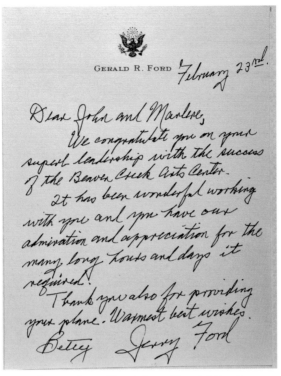

GERALD R. FORD February 23rd.

Dear John and Marlene,

We congratulate you on your superb leadership with the success of the Beaver Creek Arts Center.

It has been wonderful working with you and you have our admiration and appreciation for the many long hours and days it required!

Thank you also for providing your plane. Warmest best wishes.

Betty   Jerry Ford

Letter from President Gerald Ford

2000 – The arrival of *My Marzy*

2004 – Our 50th wedding anniversary

Cousins having a ball – June 19, 2005

More silly moments with our grandchildren

JT and I goofing around

2009 – Celebrating our 55th anniversary
with an around-the-world cruise

2009 – Celebrating my 80th birthday

Skiing in Beaver Creek

You have always been my number one, Marzy!

Marlene and I visiting my hometown in Holland

2016 – Lora, John, me, Marlene, and Kris at the Detroit Symphony
Orchestra Heroes Gala where they honored Marlene and me

2019 – Celebrating my 90th birthday

Celebrating our 65th wedding anniversary and my 90th birthday

With my sisters, Diena and Riene

Dutch – the boat named after me for my 90th birthday

"DANCING WITH LIGHT"
CASA DEL DELFINO
APRIL 26, 2019

Dancing with Light is a bronze we own that
reminds me of our love for one another

The Sugar Boll

Watch us grow – June 19, 1954

We have grown — June 2019

The painting named *Miracle* reflects the story of our lives
that started with work boots and ballet slippers

Our love for each other is still magical

A collage of our life together

"Trust Me"

made perfect sense. We wanted OPU holders to be able to vote shoulder-to-shoulder on the merger with other shareholders of the company. It just had never been done before in the context of a publicly held company."

The Chateau board didn't have an official reply from the IRS before it had to vote on Zell's revised offer, but we were confident enough to register the company's next rejection of Zell. And sure enough, though it was received a few weeks after the board's vote, while Zell was still stewing and spewing, the agency's ruling upheld the exchange that Chateau and ROC already had executed. The IRS would allow OPU holders to convert enough of their units to stock without a tax penalty.

Soon thereafter, we advised Zell that he no longer had control of the situation. With that, he had another meeting with the press and other people in New York and said on Bloomberg Television, "I've been Chateaued."

Zell indeed was defeated.

Sometime a few months before, when Zell was mounting his bid to take over my company, Levin gave me a gift in an attempt to bolster my spirits. It was a reproduction of a flag that was flown by U.S. Commodore Oliver Hazard Perry during the legendary Battle of Lake Erie during the War of 1812. "Don't Give Up the Ship," it said, its inspiring slogan coming from the last words of Captain James Lawrence who spoke them as he lay dying on his ship in battle three months before.

"We gathered for our celebration of the merger at their home in Grosse Pointe Shores, and we went into John and Marlene's lower level, and there was the flag that I had given him, unfurled and hanging over the fireplace," Levin said. "Even today, that memory gives me the chills."

⁓

Much later in his career, Zell complained to an audience, "The hardest thing to find is an honest man." He didn't mention me, but he might have added, "an honest man ... who actually fights for what he believes." If nothing else, I like to believe that I'm an honest man and that was the real undoing of Zell's acquisition bid for Chateau. Interestingly, Zell didn't mention his failed takeover bid of Chateau Properties in his 240-page book.

"John never lost his sense of direction amid this, never got angry at anybody, never blamed anybody," Levin said. "And he led us sort of like the captain of a ship in really choppy waters, through rain and storm, the waves slamming against him. And he's sailing through it, maybe with a smile on his face, because somewhere down the line he had confidence we were going to get through it. He never lost that."

In February 1997, ROC Communities shareholders overwhelmingly approved the merger with us. The new company, Chateau Communities Inc., would be based in Englewood, with Chateau's headquarters in Michigan becoming a divisional office for the new company's properties in the northeastern United States. By the time later in February that Chateau was ready to convene a special meeting of our shareholders at the Crowne Plaza Pontchartrain Hotel in downtown Detroit, the deal was all but in place.

After Chateau shareholders also overwhelmingly approved the deal, I told the *Detroit Free Press* that the saga "has been exciting. A learning experience. The kind of experience you only want to go through once in your life."

CHAPTER 14

Walking Away

AS WE HAD ENVISIONED WHEN CHATEAU
Properties merged with ROC Communities in 1997,
the combined company became enormous by the early
2000s. It now comprised of 257 communities in thirty-two states, with 70,000 rentable sites.

We were the largest mobile home operator in the country—much to the chagrin of Sam Zell—and we were the good guys. We didn't mess with anyone. We didn't do anything very complicated. We acquired a piece of land, went through the proper channels to get it zoned, and built five-star communities, where our residents enjoyed living and didn't disrupt their neighbors who had already been living there.

Over the next two years, Chateau Communities acquired mobile home parks in Connecticut, Florida, Indiana, North Carolina, and South Carolina. In Maryland, we worked with a home developer to introduce two-story manufactured homes, which included garages, porches, and, for the first time, optional basements. The development near Baltimore, called New Colony Village, even had a day care center and general store for residents. The National Manufactured Housing Congress named it the Best New Land-Lease Community. Chateau Communities was named the National Manufactured Home Community Operator of the Year for the sixth straight year.

By 1999, the company decided to shift its focus away from acquisitions as a growth strategy. We created new revenue streams by introducing services to our existing residents, including shed storage rental, prescription delivery, home health services, medical equipment rental, security systems, and even home financing and homeowners' insurance. The plan worked, as our revenues increased 9.4 percent, from $173 million in 1998 to $189.4 million in 1999.

Obviously, after the company's public stock offering in 1993 and the subsequent merger, Chateau Properties was becoming a very different company than the one I built, operating in a very different way than I was used to running it. The Chateau Estates that I built was a welcoming, family-oriented enterprise where I tried to ensure that my enthusiasm provided much of the charge each day.

"He'd walk in the office with so much energy and walk past us that we'd have to lay on our papers and hold them down as he whooshed by," said Stacy Messih, my executive assistant who also works for the Boll Foundation. "He'd give me a list of people he wanted to talk with, going from governors to presidents of organizations to sweet old widows."

And I could quickly switch gears between them. I'd yell out from my office, "Stacy, get the next one on!" [the phone].

Betty Bosch, who joined Chateau as a secretary in 1988 and still works for me today, recalled that I "would walk through and greet everyone by name, and greet guests with an energy that was always powerful. It was an amazing place to work. If we could recreate that, every one of us would say, 'Yes, let's go back there.'"

I made sure that my company also had plenty of room for people like Lot Murray, my longtime employee at Lakeview Excavating and then at my personal residence, and my brother-in-law Gene Nelson. He was the son of a Baptist preacher whom Diena met in St. Louis in 1950 during her medical training. Gene worked as a foreman for Lakeview Excavating for several years, left the company, and then was welcomed back to Chateau by me during the mid-1970s recession.

Their hard work and loyalty were exemplary of the contributions that so many individuals made in building Chateau. In turn, I demonstrated loyalty to these long-time employees all the way through the fight with Zell in which I protected their stock-like "units" of ownership. In fact, after an unfortunate accident where a Chateau truck rolled over Gene in the mid-1980s, severely damaging a shoulder, I retired my brother-in-law, who could rely for his financial future on the OPU stock he'd earned at Chateau.

But during the 1990s, that Chateau company was disappearing under the company's increasing size and new form of governance, and the varying extra forms of accountability and transparency that came with having public shareholders.

For one thing, the growth imperative was beginning to wear on me. A big part of the idea of going public in 1993 was for

Chateau to expand aggressively and quickly and overtake the rest of the industry, including Zell, to become the unprecedented 800-pound gorilla of the manufactured-home community REIT business.

But as Chateau acquired operations in far-flung jurisdictions including Arizona and California, management in general was getting more difficult. I wasn't traveling much in those days, but I was accustomed to being a hands-on owner who inspected properties, consulted with my on-site managers, and talked to the residents about what they liked and didn't like about living in our five-star communities.

It was impossible to get to every one of our communities after we acquired so many. We even had to purchase fractional ownership in a couple of corporate airplanes for our executives to keep on top of things in a business where observing the tangible, physical integrity of our facilities was crucial.

Supervision of geographic regions of the company and of individual mobile-home communities became increasingly remote from the management team I'd built, which once ensured they were run the way I wanted them to be run. The company got to the size where I didn't feel comfortable anymore. Managers were reaping profits from selling out to us and then not maintaining their properties. I was disappointed to go back and look at some of the communities; it bothered me. We had a lot of pride. But I would go back and see cars jacked up, and other things that just didn't feel right for a five-star community.

I'll be honest: having to run a publicly held company also began to wear on me. I had the typical complaints of CEOs of such companies about the required sacrifice of long-term investment to satisfy the monster of quarter-to-quarter financial expectations. We performed well enough in that arena, realizing a 14 percent average annual return on Chateau stock during the decade I was chairman, after the IPO. But for me, my objections were even more basic than that, in many ways addressed to how Chateau's culture had to change along with its reporting responsibilities.

We didn't have a lot of titles as a private company, just accountability. But being public meant we had to have a board and officers and identify people with specific roles because the public needed to have confidence in what we were doing.

After several years, Chateau's investment bankers at Merrill Lynch began to press us to diversify into apartment holdings and arranged for the purchase of one operation that held both multifamily housing complexes and mobile-home communities. I'd built some apartments separately over the years. Not many; maybe 1,000 units. But now suddenly we were going to start blending management of Chateau communities with managing apartments? I hadn't gone to college and didn't have training in this larger kind of structure.

That's when I decided I was ready to sell. I had long passed retirement age, and at seventy-three, I thought maybe I ought to take a hard look at selling. I was finally getting tired. I didn't want to keep doing what I was doing.

By then my holding in Chateau Communities was a minority share, but it was by far the largest investment anyone had in our company. So my decision to exercise my exit strategy required the company to sell itself. In 2002, Chateau advertised for help executing such a sale, and Goldman Sachs stepped up. The following May, this blue-chip investment firm set up a "war room" to entertain competing bids.

As you might have guessed, Zell tried to acquire my company once again, offering $1.82 billion, or about $26 per outstanding share. He failed a second time. The State of Washington's pension fund was the highest bidder among four offers and acquired the company for $2.3 billion, more than half of that in assumption of debt and preferred stock. The pension fund worked the deal through a company it controlled, Hometown America, a much smaller player in the mobile home industry than Chateau.

Soon the pension fund announced that it had decided to take Chateau private and as it consolidated administration under Chicago-based Hometown America, the new owners ended the two-headed arrangement that ran Chateau for a decade from offices in Macomb County and in Denver.

Of course, I wasn't very happy with the news that the State of Washington pension fund was going to take Chateau private because that would require its purchase of my stock—and the immediate requirement that I pay a large amount from my life-time investment in taxes to Uncle Sam. Fortunately, I was able to work out a fifteen-year payment schedule with Chateau's new owners, which would give me a reasonable tax on my capital gains over the next decades, which was quite a relief.

Obviously, I had never experienced anything like exiting the giant company I built over nearly a half century. I would have plenty of time for thoughts about the holistic significance of the event to my life, but right away the most jarring part about it was the dramatic change to my routine.

All of a sudden, I'm out of business and retired. The next day, I didn't have an office to go to. I'm thinking, "How come nobody is calling me? Geez." And then I really began to realize that I was out of business. I wasn't making those decisions anymore.

With so much free time on my hands, I began to look back at what I'd built and what I still wanted to build during the time I had left on Earth. I got to thinking about the word "develop." Obviously, I started out as a contractor and later branched off into real estate development. There are certain ingredients and a type of mental gymnastics a developer goes through when he or she thinks about a project. I think the same thing can be said about the development of a person, which is far more important, and that's where Marlene and I decided we wanted to focus our time and energy during retirement. We wanted to build up people and help them fulfill their best lives.

One of the first things a developer takes into account when he or she looks at a piece of property is potential. I looked at thousands of pieces of property during my career, many of which other people passed on for various reasons. While looking at the potential of a swamp or a piece of undeveloped land, the untrained eye might say, "Well, who in the world would want to fool with this thing?" But when you can visualize and use your imagination, you can see enormous potential. You might say to yourself, *This can work!*

The same thing happens with people. More than likely, somebody saw the potential in each of us somewhere down the road. I'm so glad that back in the early years that not only did God see the potential in me, so did other businessmen, who recognized the same things. It's not always easy. Sometimes as developers, we have to tear things down. There might be an old, dilapidated building on a site that needs to be razed. We can't visualize the new structure because the old one is in the way. Sometimes when we are working with people, we realize there's a lot of tearing down to do and we have to be patient. Making changes is difficult.

Like real estate development, changing others' lives also requires commitment and risk. We have to make the commitment to start and must stick with it. You'll never develop anything, whether in real estate or in helping others, if you don't put in the time. Obviously, there was considerable risk in developing mobile home communities. They were either going to make it or not. You're not going to change everyone you might want to help, and there are going to be plenty of disappointments along the way. But in God's eyes, as long as we're faithful to Him, He will do what is supposed to be done.

I spent most of my life in the development business. Marlene and I helped develop our children and our grandchildren. I can't say that I developed my wife; I think she developed me! I developed a lot of five-star communities and a few buildings. Over the years, I had some input into the lives of others, including my friends, employees, and colleagues.

As I pondered what to do in retirement, I realized I would have been a lot better off if I had spent more time in the development of lives rather than in the development of brick and mortar. Fortunately, because of God's blessings, I still had plenty of time and the resources to do it.

CHAPTER 15

The Builder at Home

BY THE EARLY 1970S, I WAS ACCUSTOMED TO
being intimately involved in anything my company
built. I'd basically built two of my own houses. I'd built
a huge company based on, yes, building developments
and communities around the country through Chateau
Properties. Through my other company, Lakeview
Excavating, I even had built some strip malls and apartment buildings in Macomb County. I was involved in
the planning, development, and construction of those
projects.

But Sugar Boll—well, that was another story.

Marlene and I, along with our three kids, loved to ski. Once Chateau was successfully off the ground, I wanted to apply some of the fruits of our labors to creating a second home at one of the handful of ski resorts in northern Michigan.

The best candidate was Sugarloaf in Leelanau County—on the "little finger" of the Michigan mitten. Sugarloaf was where each of our three kids had learned to ski, and it was becoming one of the most popular skiing destinations in the country. In those days, Sugarloaf was one of the skiing gems of the entire Midwest, offering breathtaking views of Lake Michigan, plenty of powdery snow filtering down onto its slopes, and a run or two that could test some of the most expert skiers in the world. Sugarloaf's hotel, lodge, and condos that lined the base area were regularly at capacity.

While our Chateau properties didn't offer me much of an opportunity to display my creativity, I wanted to tap into my innovative side with this house and construct something that not only would be a great gathering place for family and friends but also a testament to my capabilities as an innovative builder.

For a couple of years, Marlene and I had been taking photographs of homes we saw on skiing trips not only in Michigan but also in other parts of the country, such as Colorado and Vermont. And then we came upon an architect who lived in Suttons Bay, Michigan. We went by a couple of houses he'd built and were pleased by the different styles. We also took photos and started to make up sketches of what we would want.

Roger Hummel was the architect, and one of his designs was at Sugarloaf Mountain, not even a few hundred yards up the road from where our house eventually was built. We hired Hummel to design our dream ski home. Armed with our photos and sketches, we drove the four hours from Fraser to Suttons Bay to tell our new architect exactly what we wanted in the home that we would call Sugar Boll. As Hummel invited us into his office, he noticed I was toting a bunch of my own materials for the appointment.

"You can leave those in the car for now," Hummel told me. "Let's go inside and talk. I'd like to get the feeling for what you have in mind." For me, leaving behind my sketches for a discussion about building something would be like leaving behind the shovel when I wanted to dig a hole.

We ended up meeting with him for three or four hours, and he made some sketches, too, and showed us a few things. Then he got to the point where he said, "I think I have all the information I need from you." As we were walking out, I said, "What about my sketches?"

"I'd rather not see them," Hummel said. "Quite frankly, I have an impression of what you might like to do, and I'd rather not have it flavored by what someone else has drawn. I would rather you take them home with you."

⁓

Whether it was creating a one-of-a-kind cantilevered ski lodge in northern Michigan, pioneering an exclusive development in Colorado, or helping expand a seaside retirement community in Key Largo, we have enjoyed constructing additional homes where we could gather family members and friends around us for fun and fellowship, and launch great adventures together. And wherever we were living on a particular day, in a certain month or during any season of the year, Marlene and I continued to be all about helping build the communities that surrounded us.

Indeed, for us, constructing a new house of our own design wasn't merely about having another place, in another climate, to hang our hats, park our skis, or dock our boats. It was about becoming a part of a new community and establishing our roots among new friends and neighbors.

For instance, we were members of the Clinton River Boat Club on Lake St. Clair. The CRBC is located on a private fourteen-acre island on the Middle Channel, near the southernmost part of Harsens Island. CRBC had been founded in 1940 by a group of boat lovers, and the "club" consisted of little more than a clubhouse and docks, where members tied up for the weekend.

After Marlene and I joined the Clinton River Boat Club, I became Commodore and wanted to build tennis courts there. Of course, everyone told me it couldn't be done because you couldn't get the required equipment onto the island. I came up with a solution by putting the heavy equipment, including a cement truck, on a barge on the shore of Lake St. Clair. We used a tugboat to pull it to the island. I raised about $18,000 from the members to finance the courts, and I agreed to oversee the project.

Since I couldn't be on the island every day because of other responsibilities, Marlene had to take over. We hired laborers whom Marlene had to drive to the island on our forty-one-foot Chris-Craft boat. When she would come back down the river with no one on board, people would say, "Where did she unload them?"

———

Building Sugar Boll "by myself" wasn't going to be the case, of course, but I embraced the process, relished the project, and participated in whatever ways I could. Hummel was a very accomplished architect and had built many beautiful homes, and I understood that he was better equipped than me to design exactly what we wanted with his God-given talents.

After a few months, Hummel came back to us with a stunning design for Sugar Boll. His idea was to almost camouflage the home into the landscape, while large, frameless panes of glass—including one that was about twenty feet long—would provide unobstructed views of Lake Michigan and of the slopes. The house wasn't much more than 2,000 square feet in total, but he took advantage of every bit of space. There was plenty of seating and sleeping quarters.

In Hummel's vision, Sugar Boll would lie on the floor of its own ravine and spire skyward from a small base, cleverly canti-levered into the hill. He designed a grand fireplace out of stone. He put indirect lighting throughout the house and a chande-lier made of cedar would hang over the dining-room table. The most outstanding of the many unusual features of Sugar Boll was its unique floors, which are made out of cross-sections of branches of cherry trees. They're the feature we most remember now about a house that was built a half-century ago.

There was a door to the outside on the lowest level, so our kids and friends could descend a set of thirty cherry-log stairs cut into the slope, using the rope handrail, and rush directly out onto the ski hill. When they came back to Sugar Boll, after Marlene rang a bell on the shed to let them know it was time for lunch, there was a cozy sauna on the same level where they could warm up. There was another area strewn with stones where they could set their skis and boots to dry into a drain without creating a watery mess.

Nearly every weekend in those days, Marlene would pack the family car, including our three kids and the dogs, and we would all enjoy a couple of days of skiing. Then we'd turn around and come home on Sunday—and repeat it all again the next Friday. Sugar Boll became the place where we spent Thanksgiving and Christmas holidays, and extended-family members and friends would check in and out as well. It was the place where we made so many cherished memories as a family, and our grandchildren would eventually enjoy it as well.

By the mid-1970s, as our children got older, the area around Fraser had grown so rapidly that the schools couldn't keep up with the exploding population. At one point, the school system said the kids might have to go to half-days because there weren't enough classrooms available. So we started searching for a better place for our children to learn.

We were interested in moving to Grosse Pointe, the historic neighborhood that hugs the Lake St. Clair shoreline northeast of Detroit. Marlene and I decided that we wanted to put the kids in Grosse Pointe Academy, the premiere private school on that side of the city. So in 1978 we bought a four-bedroom, wooden-framed house on a small cul de sac in Grosse Pointe Shores.

Initially, Marlene and I believed it would only be a temporary move and that we would return to the country once our kids graduated from high school. But the kids started to make a lot of friends, and so did we, so we weren't sure we wanted to return to rural Macomb County.

Another thing began to anchor our family to Grosse Pointe was Lake St. Clair. I grew up on the lake, and Marlene lived near the Atlantic Ocean as a child. We both loved being on the water. We owned boats throughout our marriage and spent so many weekends as a family on Michigan's lakes, whether it was fishing, skiing, or just cruising up and down the Detroit River. Those were great opportunities to spend time with our children.

In 1982, Marlene and I were invited to a party at one of the exquisite homes on Lake St. Clair in the Shores. Marlene looked over at the house next door, which had recently been put up for sale. A few months later, we purchased the home at 930 Lake Shore Road. It was a 6,000-square-foot, English manor home that was originally built in 1928. The house had leaded glass windows, intricate woodwork, a front door as thick as a gravestone, an exquisite lawn leading down to the lake, more greenery than an English garden, and a finished basement with more living space alone than our first two homes put together.

In the 1980s, Marlene and I took a liking to the idea of having a third home, a permanent spot in the Rocky Mountains. Within several years, former U.S. President Gerald Ford —a Michigan native and adoptive Coloradan like me—was leading the "Surprise!" call at my birthday party. And in 1997, Marlene and I were named Beaver Creek's "Citizens of the Year."

Located in Eagle County, for decades Beaver Creek had been speculated as the site of a future ski mecca before Vail Resorts opened it to the public in 1980. We were attracted to Beaver Creek because we were looking for a way to elevate our passion for skiing. Sugarloaf and the rest of Michigan's peaks were only so high and their runs only so long, and the hills in my native state were no longer much of a challenge because of our experience.

Among other things, I believed getting in early on the development of a community could give me an important role shaping it to my liking. Confident in my own vision and experience, I saw great potential in this lovely area of the Rockies. So after a couple of years of condo ownership, we decided to build a house at Beaver Creek and leapt into a development by Frank Stronach, who had built Magna Corporation into a huge auto supplier in Canada. There were eight home sites.

Bertil Hult became our neighbor. Bertil was an entrepreneur who massaged a brilliant idea into a highly successful company over the decades. A native Swede, Bertil struggled with dyslexia and learned to speak English as a high-school dropout in London while serving as a gofer for a shipbroker. After eventually returning to school, Bertil founded the language-teaching company EF Education—at the age of 23, in his university dormitory in Lund, Sweden. Over a half-century beginning in 1965, Bertil moved from one country in Europe to another and built EF into a massive company with 55,000 employees and dominance of his industry.

When he and his wife moved to California in 1983, Bertil took his fondness for skiing with him, soon eyeing Beaver Creek as a place he might want to have a home. As luck would have it, we both arrived at the site where we wanted to build our house at the same time with different realtors.

Bertil looked at me and said, "You were here first, you pick your site first." I picked mine, and he picked one right next to us. That's how we became friends.

Serendipitously, Stronach named his development The Chateau, and we called our house at Beaver Creek Chateau des Montagnes, meaning "home in the mountains." When Stronach announced this familiar name for the development during a board meeting, I joked with my friend by reaching into my pocket, pulling out a pocketknife, and sliding it down the table to him. It bore the name and logo of Chateau Estates. "You should have asked me and saved yourself the expense of a PR firm," I quipped.

Along with many others, we became active in helping create the community. Peter May, a Coloradan and New York investment banker, and our neighbor in Beaver Creek helped build up the community. Some of my friends there even started calling me "the father of Beaver Creek." Of course, I tried to work behind the scenes, and never sought out credit for what I was doing, but we loved the place so much. It was so beautiful, and the skiing was tremendous, and we wanted our friends to be able to enjoy it as well.

We were instrumental in designing and raising funds for the Vilar Performing Arts Center in Beaver Creek that opened in 1998 and has become a prime amenity for the community. The cause drew Marlene's attention as well as mine because she was always looking for opportunities to promote the arts.

We also received very welcome help from President Ford, who was himself active in Beaver Creek and a member of the foundation board along with Marlene. And so, few were shocked outside of me to see the seventy-six-year-old former president lead the cheers for me when I walked into May's house in June 1989 for what turned out to be a surprise celebration of my sixtieth birthday. Nine years later, Ford and I were comparing surgical knees at the grand opening gala for the Vilar Performing Arts Center.

———

Ocean Reef was another place where I had to rely on my vision for development to see the future—and to help my family see what I foresaw. Ocean Reef was a barely dry, undeveloped outpost at the northern end of the Florida Keys, just south of the islands of Biscayne National Park and, from fabled Key Largo, in the opposite direction from Key West.

The first time we went to the island, it was still basically a little fishing village with a grocery store and homes. There also was a huge problem with no-see-ums, a kind of biting bug—so bad that many people thought this swampy area could never be developed.

The key to our interest in Ocean Reef, oddly enough, lay in the oil of the chrysanthemum plant. Some chemist developed a bug antidote by squeezing the oil of the chrysanthemum bud, and the substance spread like wildfire. Planes would dump chrysanthemum dust on the island to keep insects at bay and, gradually, Ocean Reef attracted more and more people who were serious about building homes there.

Just a few minutes' boat ride to the southwest, the magnetic effect of Key Largo, of course, helped a lot. On one of our many boating excursions to the area, we became members of the fabled, century-old Anglers Club in North Key Largo. The Anglers' walls are plastered with the family flags of members and with memorabilia from decades past.

By 2005, Marlene and I decided to make an investment in Ocean Reef. We built a waterside home and our first challenge, like our neighbors, was meeting local building codes that were meant to make sure houses could withstand hurricanes. Builders had to put 164 supports under our house, some of which descended forty feet below until they found bedrock. Concrete and steel rods fill those holes and support the structure.

Our builders, architects, and interior designers built us a beautiful home on the water, with a sprawling pool and hot tub on a backyard veranda that overlooks the bay. However, my favorite feature is a 1,500-gallon aquarium in the living room that is encased by one-and-one-half-inch-thick glass in a convex shape, because the water pressure is so high that it would shatter a straight piece of glass.

The fascinating slice of nature features hundreds of fish, shrimp, and other creatures, including dozens of vibrantly colored fish and live coral imported from Africa. A caretaker visits our home three times a week to make sure the food chain in the aquarium is working the way nature intended, and to inspect the attached equipment room in the basement, which is as large as a typical American bedroom. Algae for feed is grown in the downstairs room, and the fish are fed automatically. A lighting system mimics changes from day through night.

In so many ways, our home in Ocean Reef, Casa del Delfino, became another home away from home for us. Our family and friends have enjoyed boating, fishing, golf, and delicious seafood dinners on our back veranda. Like Sugar Boll and Chateau des Montagnes, it has become a place for our family and friends to make so many indelible memories.

CHAPTER 16

Captain John

MY ANCESTORS MADE THEIR LIVING FROM THE sea in the Netherlands, and my clan ended up settling on the Great Lakes when they came to America, so it was only natural for me to have a close relationship with the water. From the time I was able to afford my first small boat until I worked my way up to buying an Italian-built, 115-foot Benetti yacht that I named after Marlene, *My Marzy*, I was an avid sailor, as much at home on the water as I was on land. Marlene fit capably and enthusiastically into that world.

As a couple, with family members, and friends, our treks have been as short as fifteen minutes of water skiing on Lake St. Clair or as relaxed as months-long journeys along fascinating coastlines that provided hundreds of micro-experiences along the way. We have sailed among the sparkling beauty of Canada's Georgian Bay and the eastern lobe of Lake Huron, which doesn't appear on American maps of the Great Lakes, where it looks as though God opened His hand and scattered pebbles that became thousands of small islands. We've toured the Mediterranean, a cradle of civilization where ancient navies battled. And we've explored the ins and outs of the bright blue waters of the Caribbean.

As surely as we have charted the births of our grandchildren and the groundbreakings of our new homes, Marlene and I have tracked the progress of our lives through the couple dozen boats we have enjoyed, their types, names, lengths, and capabilities— and the many memories they have provided.

For we understand how being at sea can provide perspectives, insights, and experiences that are unparalleled on land. We wanted our children and friends to experience that with us. When our daughter Kristine and her future husband, Jim Mestdagh, graduated from college, Jim told me he had to find a job. I told him that can wait. He was going to have the next forty or fifty years to work. Instead, I took him sailing for a month.

My boats also have served as platforms where I could satisfy my thirst for adventure and, at times, demonstrate bravado. To a great extent, it was in, on, and even behind boats where the legend of "Trust Me John Boll" was born.

Actually, my biggest nautical accomplishment occurred on dry land, at the Grosse Pointe Yacht Club, a fabled institution that sits on a man-made piece of land jutting into Lake St. Clair on its western shore, off Lake Shore Road in Grosse Pointe Shores and not far from our home. In 1986, I became Commodore—the elected layperson in charge of the club—and I immediately went to work.

The club dates to 1914 when two dozen men formed an association to pursue their interests in ice boating and sailing on the lake. They included Edsel Ford, son of Henry Ford, who later would build a famous mansion barely a mile from the club and just up the road from the house we eventually owned. Not coincidentally, Clarence Ayers, the original owner of our home, played a key role in the formation of GPYC, donating as its site a parcel of land he had recently purchased. Club founders worked with the city to fill in the point at the intersection of Lake Shore and Vernier roads and put a community park next door to the club.

Guy Lowell, a Boston architect and yachtsman, designed the GPYC clubhouse, which was dedicated on the Fourth of July in 1929—just a few months before the infamous stock market crash in October. As a result of the crash, the club went bankrupt in 1934. It eventually reopened behind a cut-rate entry fee of just $1,000. The club was placed on the National Register of Historic Places in 2014.

I admired the grand institution almost from my youth, but the relationship was from afar—and just a dream to become a member. I would glide past the clubhouse on my small sailboats in the summer, or race nearby on iceboats in the winter. As Marlene likes to say, "If you weren't part of the Grosse Pointe Yacht Club, you were in awe of it."

You have to understand that back then there were St. Clair Shores people and there were Grosse Pointe people, supposedly. We would look at the Grosse Pointe Yacht Club and go, "Wow!" We didn't get close to it; we didn't feel we deserved to be that close. It was just a feeling, maybe out of respect for the grandest yacht club in the entire country. I finally got that feeling under control, and got closer and closer to the club, until I finally got involved.

Our family joined the club after we moved to Grosse Pointe Shores in 1978. The next year, we hosted our twenty-fifth wedding anniversary party for 200 people at the club. Over the next several years, I would like to think that I became an influential member of GPYC.

Indeed, much like I had done at Clinton River Boat Club and would later do at Beaver Creek and Ocean Reef, I tried to make the yacht club a better place. For instance, in 1982 GPYC acquired a 112-foot-long, metal, tapered flagpole from Rose Terrace, the estate of Anna Thompson Dodge, who was the widow of Horace E. Dodge Sr.—one of Detroit's legendary "Dodge Brothers." Club elders wanted to place the storied flagpole prominently in front of the building. But because the pole had been simply sawed off at ground level several years earlier at the Dodge estate and then stored, the club struggled with how to take advantage of the full and marvelous height of the pole and avoid having to bury any significant portion of it to stabilize it.

I came up with a solution, designing a sort of cradle for the flagpole that ensured only an earthquake could disengage it. I had a six-foot hole dug for the pole into which eight steel rods were driven, more than fifty feet into the ground, which were then capped with six feet of concrete. Workers welded the pole to a steel base plate and bolted it to the steel rods, then welded four fins to the bottom of the pole and the base plate for further stability. The GPYC flag was placed atop the pole.

By the mid-1980s, some significant structural issues arose at the club, including a kitchen that was hopelessly outdated and way too small to service the kind of crowds that were gathering there. County authorities had been kind to let things go as long as they had. Then the big recessions of 1980 and 1982 rocked the club's automotive-related membership base. I was able to raise some capital from members to shore up the club financially, so we were able to make the much-needed improvements.

There also was the issue of rising Lake St. Clair water levels that were putting significant hydrologic pressure underneath the structure, threatening the club's basement and more. With my excavating experience and engineering mind, I was able to come up with—and then supervise execution of—additional structural cementing of the basement floor that keeps the lake at bay to this day.

Those projects must have proved I was the right man for the top job, and club directors elected me commodore in 1986. Righting the Grosse Pointe Yacht Club out of the recessions provided a challenging task for me, combining my passion for boating with the organizational challenges and rewards of restoring this revered institution.

In fact, I put up about $100,000 of my own money in 1986 for the kitchen expansion and renovation, as an advance to GPYC, and only after that did I recruit other members to kick in their own contributions.

Much like Clinton River Boat Club and Sugar Boll, Marlene and I also used GPYC as a platform for family building. John Jr. worked with me on our boats and cleaned other members' crafts. Kristine played tennis, and Lora made the club swim team. When she had practices at 6 a.m., often our entire family would stay on our boat in the club's marina so Lora almost literally could roll out of bed and into the water. The club afforded us another great opportunity to spend time with our children and friends.

The water proved to be a great proving ground for me partly because early on I'd taken to the deep blue like a fish. When my sisters and I were still kids, our father, Anton, managed to scrape together the funds for a fifteen-foot boat with a cloth sail. My first boat was a twenty-four-foot Chris-Craft kit I built in 1956. Six years later, our family stretched our thin household budget to graduate to a thirty-two-foot sailboat, a fiberglass craft built by the legendary Owens Boat Company in Maryland.

For several years, we also scurried about on our first power-boat, an eighteen-footer, *Rockette*, which we would trailer to northern Michigan. In 1969, we bought a thirty-six-foot Chris-Craft powerboat we christened *Al Mar*, enjoying trips on it to Georgian Bay in each of the next few summers with family members and friends, picking wild blueberries and enjoying island-hopping. I taught Marlene how to handle the boat so when I had to return to Detroit to work, she and the kids could stay until I came back.

In 1978, I added a new forty-seven-foot sailboat to head the Boll fleet, christened *GolfDanzer*, and helmed the boat on its maiden voyage. Our family sailed from St. Petersburg, Florida, where the boat was built, to the Grosse Pointe Yacht Club over a period of a few months spanning the spring and summer. The objective was to slice triumphantly into Lake St. Clair by the Fourth of July.

Unfortunately, I quickly decided I didn't particularly like how the vessel performed. It was a sailboat that also, with a motor, was a powerboat—a hybrid that failed at both. But *GolfDanzer* served as the vehicle for our family's long trip up and around the East Coast, with plenty of stops along the way where the kids executed "school exchanges." We got to the yacht club on the Fourth of July just as all the activities were starting.

Soon we graduated to a fifty-three-foot sailboat that I ordered from Ted Hood, a boat builder in Massachusetts. After two years our Little Harbor sailboat, which we named *Zeedanzer* for its place of construction, was ready for us to pick up. A new adventure ensued as we navigated the route down through Long Island Sound, up the Hudson River, and westward through the Erie Barge Canal, which was built in 1825 to establish a navigable waterway from New York City and the Atlantic Ocean to the Great Lakes.

To get to Lake Erie and an easy jaunt back to Grosse Pointe, *Zeedanzer* had to negotiate a 363-mile trip on the canal punctuated by forty locks that gradually lift boats up the 600-foot incline to the Great Lakes Basin from sea level at the Atlantic. Our kids played a crucial role in getting *Zeedanzer* through ancient locks that were built to assist commercial vehicles, not pleasure boats.

They would climb the steps and hold our boat to the side of the lock with the lines. We also had to take down the mast, which was sixty feet high, to get through some of the locks, and we couldn't put the mast back on again until we got to Toledo. It took a lot of effort to get us back home.

Our boat-building tourism got ever more elaborate. In 1985, for example, Marlene and I flew to Hong Kong and then on to Taiwan to see a new sailboat being made there for us. Then there was the ultimate: taking delivery in Italy of the 115-foot Benetti cruiser, *My Marzy*, and putting the yacht through its first paces on the Mediterranean.

My Marzy was going to be the ultimate expression of my love affair with seagoing vessels, but that wasn't just because it would be the largest boat we ever owned. More than that, I was going to approach the construction of my Benetti superyacht as if it were the first Chateau community or one of my new homes: I wasn't going to be a passive buyer. And with my role at my company winding down, I could devote enough time to play a serious role in how *My Marzy* was put together.

When we chose Benetti, we were given a lot of freedom with the design of the boat. Our design tweaks ranged from converting two of the staterooms into one larger, more comfortable VIP suite to adding polished cherrywood beams to the ceilings in the salon, living area, and dining room. We designed a marble shower in the center of the master bathroom dividing the space into his and her sections. I also stipulated in a contract different limits for stateroom noise levels, keeping *My Marzy* very quiet.

And as in every space where we lived significant minutes of our lives, we sought to have *My Marzy* reflect some of our lifelong passions. We even got our interior designer, D.J. Kennedy, involved in the process. We wanted specific kinds of commissioned artwork that matched the ship's décor; Marlene called for a bronze sculpture of a Spanish ballerina.

After fourteen months of construction, Benetti completed *My Marzy* in July 2000. Upon taking delivery, we spent four months cruising the Mediterranean, visiting Sardinia, Sicily, and each Riviera: Italian, Spanish, and French. It was the adventure of a lifetime.

If you haven't figured it our yet, our boats are more than mere playthings—they are platforms for relationship building. Marlene and I love to take our family and friends out on our boats, not just for the immediate pleasure of it but in hopes that the vessels and what they experience on them serve as one more way to weave us together with our loved ones.

My grandson, JT Mestdagh, recalls being on the top deck of *My Marzy* at the port in Viareggio, a seaside city in Tuscany, where we had taken delivery of the yacht with six-year-old JT performing the christening. He calls me "Papi," and we were overlooking outdoor diners at the cafes from the third deck of the massive boat.

JT took out this laser pointer that I'd picked up in one of the shops, and we were shooting the pointer down as kids and other people tried to chase this red dot around. No one really knew where the light was coming from. I was just trying to do something fun with my grandson.

Also on that trip, I pulled another prank on JT with a frozen fish eyeball. Without telling anyone, I put it in JT's drink at dinner on *My Marzy*. I acted clueless until someone shockingly noticed it floating in the drink. Relentless, I then took the fish eyeball, wrapped it in paper towel, and put it in JT's bed. "It melted all over the bed," JT recalled. Then he winked. "Nani loved that."

From a very early age, Marlene and I got our children and grandchildren used to the water so they would be comfortable in and around it their entire lives. There was the big pool at the house on Millar Road, of course. On the islands of Lake St. Clair, we taught them how to dive. "Trust me," I would say.

"Because Papa and my dad were water lovers, we spent a lot of time jumping into the lake or the pool," said Alexandra, John Jr.'s daughter. "Nana and Papa would start us off by kneeling near the deep end, putting our hands together like a prayer, and leaning forward, into the water. Progressively, they taught us how to do that standing, then kneeling on the diving board, standing on the diving board, and so on. It was a progressive lesson of trust in learning how to dive. And we had some awesome diving and cannonball competitions!"

We similarly got the grandchildren involved with boating at a young age, and JT is now a fully certified 100-ton captain himself. Jim often was my partner on nautical "trust me" adventures. One time, we were venturing on *The Rockette*, my 63-foot Sea Ray powerboat, from GPYC all the way north through Lake Huron, west through the Mackinac Straits, and then southwest through Lake Michigan to the Harbor Springs resort. We left with a full tank of 1,000 gallons of fuel in the fast boat that could pierce 40 knots.

When we were coming up on Mackinac Island, Jim said, "John, maybe we should get some fuel. There aren't any fuel stops after that until Harbor Springs."

"No, we're good," I told him. "Trust me."

We kept motoring along. After a while, I told Jim to take the wheel.

"I've got to go to the bathroom again," I told him. "Besides, I don't want to be behind the wheel when we run out of fuel."

We pulled into Harbor Springs with fifty gallons left out of 1,000—we made it by a hiccup.

Jim and JT have assisted in my favorite hobby by monitoring construction of my later and larger boats, which were always being put together carefully by skilled artisans at ports halfway around the world. For our latest yacht, a fifty-five-foot Zeelander, JT and the captain of the boat flew to Holland and even went along on sea trials of the vessel with a Zeelander captain before the company shipped the boat by freighter to Baltimore.

Boat after boat, throughout our sixty-seven years of marriage, I had named every one for Marlene in some form or fashion, even in different languages. But with the Zeelander, as I turned ninety years old, I decided it was time to name a boat for myself. I christened it *Dutch*, as a tribute to the place where my ancestors first fell in love with the sea.

CHAPTER 17

"Marzy, Why Don't You Write a Letter?"

NO COUPLE LASTS AN ASTONISHING SIXTY-seven years of marriage without a solid understanding of their relationship. For Marlene and me, that under-standing is embodied in a painting we proudly display in our home, of a pair of Army boots slumped next to a pair of ballet slippers.

The painting of the boots and the ballet slippers wasn't commissioned by either of us for thousands of dollars as a Valentine's Day or anniversary gift—or anything else. We just happened to see the painting lit up in the window of a New York gallery while we were dining out during a vacation to the Big Apple. It was titled "Miracle." The painting's price was only $300, but it is priceless to us because everything about it embodies the story of our relationship—Marlene's grace, beauty, and career as a dancer, and my blue-collar beginnings in the Army and construction industry.

I think Bob Henley, our chaplain in residence at The Chapel on Ocean Reef, might have described most accurately what the painting means to us. "John is still that soldier, sitting in the front row of the theater and watching the Rockettes and waving his handkerchief to Marlene. He's still enthralled with that girl, and she with him."

There's no question that our marriage has lasted nearly seven decades because we love each other as much today as we did when we were married in that New Jersey church on June 19, 1954. If anything, our love for each other is even stronger after we've endured the ups and downs of raising a family, building businesses, and spending nearly every day of our golden years together.

"Fortunately, when John laid his eyes on Marlene, she ended up having similar drive, energy, and moral fiber that John had," said Herbert, our good friend. "It's a very special thing."

I think it's probably easier for those who know us best— our children, grandchildren, closest friends, and longtime employees and colleagues—to describe why our relationship has withstood the test of time and blossomed for so long. I only know that our marriage worked because we loved, respected, and trusted each other and had open communication. We tried to inspire, encourage, and advise each other in building our relationship. In fact, I don't remember an occasion in which we were argumentative or raised our voices at each other. I listened to Marlene, and she listened to me. We vowed to be there for each other, in sickness and in health, for better or worse, and that's exactly what we've done.

Tamara Fischer, who worked as chief financial officer for Chateau Properties for many years, said we "are as tight as two partners can be. They totally respect each other's strengths, which are very different strengths. Marlene is super practical but very artistic, and John—if he had a higher-education degree, he would have been an engineer. That's how his mind works."

Without a doubt, our relationship starts with the most important fundamental: Marlene and I believe our great marriage is an outcome of God's will for us and an expression of His love for each of us. Our son John Jr. noted that we have a "biblically based marriage that has really given them a wonderful sixty-seven years together."

Throughout our marriage, when we were faced with tragedies such as my mother's death or difficult times in business, Marlene and I relied on our faith and the Scripture. It is the same way with our marriage. God's love for us is unconditional, and the Bible tells us that we are called to imitate God, to be just like Him: "Dear friends, since God so loved us, we also ought to love one another." (1 John 4:11 NIV)

Ned Allen, who became my business partner in the 1990s when Chateau Properties bought his company, said of Marlene and me, "You can only tell so much from a distance, but they are very sincere and deeply founded in their faith, and it has been all-encompassing. So that gets played out in their relationship. It's hard to believe that they ever had a serious mistrust in their marriage or even a serious weakness. Every marriage has to go through that, but if it happened with them, it sure wasn't obvious."

Few people have known us as much as Mike Timmis and his wife, Nancy, whom we met at President Ronald Reagan's second inaugural ball in January 1985. Mike remembered that we were the only other couple dancing at the ball. Over subsequent decades, we cruised together around Cape Horn in South America, into the Baltics, up the Kiel Canal in Germany, and out into the North Sea to Stockholm. We went skiing together in Beaver Creek. And so on—to the point where we've spent thousands of hours with one another.

"They've been partners in every sense of the word," Mike Timmis said. "Her tremendous care for John, and his for her—they really have a true partnership. At an event honoring John, I once said, 'I can't think of John without thinking of Marlene, and vice versa.' When I think of them, I just think of them as 'John and Marlene.' It's always been that way."

While growing up around us at the Clinton River Boat Club, Steve Grekin observed our marriage and described us as "outstanding role models for marriage. And if they love you and you're part of their circle, they take that role very seriously."

Tyra Bone, a contemporary of our daughter Kristine and another lifetime friend of the family, noted our "mutual submission to each other that makes for a great marriage—they exemplify that 100 percent." Bone referred to dictionaries in which a definition of a word or an identification of a famous person often is accompanied by a picture next to the entry.

"If there were an entry for 'what marriage is supposed to be,' " Bone said, "John and Marlene's picture would be right there next to it."

Certainly we formed a strong partnership early on in our relationship and strengthened it from there, taking on complementary roles in the interests of building a life whose prospects, we always believed, exceeded whatever means we had at the moment.

"They truly worked together," said John Jr. "Dad worked during the day, and Mom did the books for the business and taught dance and did whatever else she needed to do to keep things moving forward and allow Dad to prosper out in the field." As Kristine pointed out, Marlene's help literally included "hosing Dad down in the garage at the end of muddy days of digging." There's no question I couldn't have built the business without her—and our family wouldn't have flourished without her sacrifices.

As for many a man building a career in post-World War II America, there were long stretches when I wasn't around much. I would leave early in the morning, work very long hours, clock in for dinner, and then repeat the cycle, often working on Saturdays as well. That's the way it was back then.

"I had to be strong," Marlene said, "because I had to get up at 4:30 a.m. and he would leave, and many times I wouldn't see him again until 8 p.m. There were a lot of prayers, a lot of dinners left sitting in the oven."

Sometimes zoning meetings and other requirements of building my business would take me away for an entire evening. Fortunately, for many years, Grandma Miller was there to help out too. Obviously, I didn't want to be away from Marlene and the kids, but it's what I had to do to make the company successful and provide for my family.

Marlene was as much of an authority figure at home as I was, and we divided parenting duties equally as much as we could. We always had a united front with the kids and never elevated our disagreements in front of them.

However, that doesn't mean we weren't above nudging each other. With expectations shaped differently from mine, partly by her experience in show business, Marlene "had higher expectations in some things than John," observed my sister Diena. "Like dress: She would look at John and say, 'That doesn't go together.' She put on all the finishing touches; she polished him. He has the shovel and the wheelbarrow, and she has the finesse."

Over time, like many couples we also could communicate effectively without saying a word. This is a skill noticed by our married grandchildren. Hopefully, we were role models for them as they begin their families. "They accomplish things without openly communicating," said our granddaughter, Alexandra.

Justin Mazza, one of our other married grandchildren, added, "They're just very in tune with each other, whether there's silence or not."

Our grandson JT observed that we "complement each other very well. Papi is quiet, and listens, and Nani listens, too, but she's more vocal. He is great at listening to her too—then he'll roll his eyes at you."

Another device that has enabled us to coexist happily for so long is that each of us became more accepting of the other's strengths and weakness. For instance, Marlene is smart and determined, and over the years she has observed tendencies in me she'd like to check, such as taking too much risk in situations, or pushing my playfulness perhaps a bit too far. Yet at the same time, Marlene has such fundamental respect for me, and the way I think, that she'll pick only certain spots to express her reservations.

For my part, when Marlene chooses to speak up, I certainly listen, understanding and appreciating this attribute of my wife—but that doesn't mean I'll always agree with her.

Our family members have seen this dynamic play out many times. One of my favorite ways to keep dinners lively with our kids and grandchildren is to poke them under the table, sometimes using a prank fork with an extending handle, other times simply squeezing a victim's leg above the kneecap to get a reflexive reaction. "You'd either have some sort of vocal outburst or shoot out of your seat," Alexandra said. "That, in turn, would prompt a look at Papa from Nana that you'd never want to get."

Our friend Jack Sullivan, the longtime general manager of the Grosse Pointe Yacht Club, also has observed this interaction between us many times. He was married to his wife for forty-seven years before she died several years ago, so Jack has a valuable perspective on what it takes to make loving relationships last over the long term.

"When John needed to be directed or something had to be strongly suggested to him, Marlene would do that," Sullivan said. "And John would always say, 'Yes, dear.' There was no way he was going to be ignoring her. At the same time, he is a strong individual, and if he felt she was incorrect, he would say, 'I'm sorry, dear, but this isn't going to fly.' They've had such mutual understanding and respect and love for each other that neither would offer up something that was too far out of the realm of what the other would want."

As Alexandra put it, "They don't fight. And she's the queen." I couldn't have said it better myself.

One of our favorite bits of communication could be called, "Marzy, why don't you write a letter?" I often have said this to my wife after she makes an observation or raises a concern she'd like to see addressed by someone, whether it's city hall, a contractor, a TV news host, a family member, a neighbor— whomever is the protagonist involved.

Like clockwork, I acknowledge her concern or accolade, listen to her express and explain her thoughts, usually affirm that it's something that could or should be addressed, and then help her take action in a manner she's familiar with.

"Whether it's a social cause, or about the arts, or education, she'll just sit quietly and you can see her get flustered about something, and the wheels start turning," said Alexandra. "She'll just go off; it's pretty great to listen to. And Papa will let her go. He's silent for a while. Then he'll say, 'Marzy, you should write a letter.' It's comical to see."

The predictability of what I will ultimately say to her, however, doesn't undermine the seriousness of Marlene's intent nor my understanding of what might happen next. For very often, Marlene does just that: She writes a letter. " 'If that's how you feel,' she always says, 'then write a letter,' " said JT. "She writes a lot of letters."

And I'm very proud to say that Marlene has corrected a lot of wrongs over the decades, from slight to significant, by expressing her opinion, urging action, and seeing her initiative through until she gets results.

"I chauffeur them a lot, and sometimes a road will be bumpy from a lot of potholes," said Ed DeWalls, our long-time gardener and family assistant in Grosse Pointe Shores. "She'll say, 'If they'd fixed this road three years ago, it would have been fine.' And John will say to her, 'Marzy, maybe you should write a letter.' And she'd say, 'I've written a letter before—and it works.' "

Marlene has roped others besides me into her letter-writing initiatives. Stacy Messih said that Marlene occasionally has called her when she's watching television in the evening, asking Messih to take notes and write a letter the next day.

"One time she was watching and saw a credit card commercial for Capital One in which they used the phrase, 'damned shame,' and she didn't like it," Messih said. "She said, 'I don't think that is appropriate. There are children and families watching TV, and watching commercials, and he could have said what he wanted to say without using that kind of language.' "

Kristine picked up the story. "So we wrote a complaint letter and shipped it off, and sure enough, the next time we saw the ad, the rest was the same, but Capital One took that phrase out. And my mom takes full credit. She's sure no one else would have written a letter. But she believes that if she doesn't speak up, no one else would."

At the same time, Marlene takes pen to paper to give praise as well. "She'll be the first to write a note or a card of congratulations," Messih said. "Or if we see a newspaper article honoring a friend, she'll cut it out and send a note to them."

One time Marlene wrote a letter to Mike Lindell, the "My Pillow" guy who has been advertising profusely on Fox News for a few years, praising the Minnesota-based entrepreneur for his very public embrace of his Christian faith. "She said," Bone recalled, " 'I love it whenever someone is willing to be true to his faith, especially in front of a bunch of people on national TV.' "

It's not always letters that Marlene sends, especially in the digital age; Marlene knows her way around an e-mail as well. And sometimes, what she wants only requires a simple phone call.

"There was an incident recently," said Anton Boll, another one of our grandchildren. "The water has been getting higher and higher on Lake St. Clair, meaning that boats have been able to get closer and closer to the shoreline of their home on the lake. That means the music they play gets louder and louder. One time when I was there for lunch, it took Nana only a few seconds to decide she wasn't going to put up with it any longer. She was quiet, but then she got up and it didn't take her more than a few seconds to make a phone call."

Marlene called the U.S. Coast Guard. The Coast Guard called the local law enforcement. Soon the music from the boats offshore was much, much quieter. And thanks to efforts by Marlene and our neighbors, in 2021 they pushed for a new ordinance to push partying boats no less than 300 feet offshore.

For Marlene and me, togetherness may be the most essential quality of our relationship. "Everything they do," said Diena, "they do together."

In the old days, amid the busyness of our lives, we had to catch togetherness on the fly many times, whether it was on Sunday drives through Chateau properties, short outings on the boat, or skiing vacations. "That's one reason Papi never got too much into golf, because he wasn't going to take off on some boys' weekend playing golf," JT said. "With them, it was always a family weekend or a couples' adventure."

Nowadays, it's common for us to sit in the evening and watch Fox News with each other or plot ways to get family and friends together with us at one of our homes or on our boat, *Dutch*.

There's an uncommon art to being able to spend this much time together, our loved ones say—and not everyone can do it. "Neither is intolerant of the other," observed our family friend George Clark. "Normally with a couple, you will have someone who's intolerant of something about the other person, but I've never seen that with John and 'Marr.' They're like a perfect match."

Having fun is another hugely important ingredient in what makes our marriage work. Our daughter Lora recalled "constant teasing and laughing between them" when she was growing up in our home. Henley, our local chaplain at Ocean Reef, cited my birthday party at a club there, where Billy Dean and Dawn, a South Florida dance band, were stringing together familiar tunes.

"Marlene gets him out on the dance floor, and he has on a little black hat with gold glitter that says, 'Happy 88th Birthday,' " Bob said. "Some people are the life of the party like Marlene, but John also reflects that life and joy he's having at the moment. She throws the party; he enjoys the party."

And, added Kristine in the same conversation, her dad "goes with it anytime Mom pulls him up there on the dance floor. 'My Marlene,' he says. They're more in love today than ever."

Maybe that's the main reason our relationship has aged like a fine wine. In his pastoral role with a big congregation of elderly members, Bob has observed that "some people fall into bitterness as they experience losses of different kinds that are just inevitable. But John and Marlene are handling their aging with grace. They know maybe that they can't go back out on the dance floor anymore, but that's alright. There's something else."

There's no doubt that I've been the luckiest man in the world. As Alexandra put it, "Everything they do and the values they have and the relationship they have—who wouldn't want sixty-seven years of that?"

CHAPTER 18

Spiritual Gifts

FOR MARLENE AND ME, FAITH IN GOD IS TRULY foundational. Our fundamental beliefs lead to behaviors that lead to disciplines that lead to habits that lead to a lifestyle that demonstrates and carries out our faith—and often results in blessings we share with others. Our pursuit of our faith also often turns routine encounters into moments of spiritual discovery that change our lives—and others'.

One of those moments was when I met Mike Timmis and his wife, Nancy, at the Reagan inaugural ball. That encounter led to bigger things for both of us, Mike recalled.

"We knew who each other were from Detroit, so they came over to our table," Mike recalled. "It wasn't long before John was asking me what was the most important thing in my life, and I said, 'My relationship with Jesus.' So he said, 'Let's sit down and talk.' "

It wasn't long after that we started a prayer group of five couples, both Protestants and Catholics, which stayed together for more than thirty years, meeting and praying for our community at least once a month.

Mike and Nancy are Catholic, and we have enjoyed a deep spiritual connection with them that weaved its way through many things over the decades. I helped Mike lead the Grosse Pointe observation of the annual National Day of Prayer Breakfast each May. In 1976, we put our shoulders into helping stage the Billy Graham Crusade at the Silverdome, the 80,000-seat stadium in Pontiac, Michigan. Thirteen years later, our families traveled to the Philippines and attended the Billy Graham Lausanne II Conference on World Evangelism, a trip that launched our many other travels together.

Mike sat on the board of Chuck Colson's Prison Fellowship ministry, and Marlene and I made a financial contribution to help that great mission. When Colson thanked us in a letter, he shared the story of an inmate his ministry was helping. She was a mother of two and was serving a twenty-two-year prison sentence for dealing drugs and gang-related crimes.

She said, "I've learned so much about my life, myself and how to deal with the daily struggles of life. I have learned if you don't put God first and trust in Him you will face many hardships. You must learn to turn your life over to God to find a true sense of peace."

The woman was released after serving twelve years, and Chuck wrote that she was a "completely different person—changed from the inside by the love and grace of Jesus Christ." Our foundation, The John A. and Marlene L. Boll Foundation, made a $1 million donation for a new building for prison fellowship in Mike's honor.

"They live out their faith day by day in a totally consistent way," Mike said. "I've been evangelizing for many years, in many different ministries, and the No. 1 thing I look for in leadership is consistency. They're two of the most consistent people I've ever met in their love for the Lord and in their pursuit of His teachings."

Despite being raised in different backgrounds, Mike and I quickly became brothers in Christ. "We came to realize we're of the same faith, though it's manifested in different ways," he said. "The fact that we grew together as brothers and sisters is something that I hope continues until the day I go to be with the Lord, and I think they do, too."

———

Religious identification began early for Marlene and me. My family was staunchly Dutch Reform, and Marlene's upbringing was Methodist. Both sets of parents had strict rules, and not consorting with Catholics was one of them. Marlene couldn't date Catholic boys growing up, her father determined—even though her mother had maintained her Catholic faith. As I told you earlier, my sister Diena had created huge drama in our house by insisting on dating a Catholic boy against our parents' wishes.

Reid Nelson, Diena's son, is the pastor in the Boll clan, having headed the congregation of a small church in Mackinaw City, Michigan, for nearly forty years. Like any good clergyman, he knows family spiritual histories aren't always influential when it comes to individual decisions about faith. Nelson has documented our personal testimonies, which is something he likes to do for everyone in our extended family.

"Uncle John didn't really give me a date when he embraced his faith, but it was in the 1940s, and he said he came to a personal relationship with Jesus Christ and that he had a personal walk with the Lord and knew Christ as his Savior," Reid said.

However, I will admit that the murder of my mother when I was thirty-two years old was a tremendous spiritual setback for me. I was amazed by how my father, Anton—while greatly saddened and saddled with the realization that his life never would be the same—accepted my mother's loss as somehow in the will of God, as something he would only understand on the other side of mortality. Yet I struggled to understand why something so tragic would happen to our family.

As people comforted my father, he would say, "It's the Lord's will, and I'm prepared to accept it." I heard that again and again. And when he stood there and said that to people, they couldn't argue with that. That's how he got through those days.

But I wrestled with my emotional and spiritual pain, often meeting with Pastor Leslie Crain of our family's church at that time, Lakeshore Presbyterian in St. Clair Shores, to help work through it. It took me three years to get past it and understand it myself.

Of course, I relied on my faith in Christ to get me through that difficult time. You only have to watch the evening news to know that bad things are happening all over the world, each and every day. God didn't create evil. But He did create man— and He gave us free will. Fortunately, we have a God that loves us. He sent His only son to suffer for us, and His Holy Spirit to comfort us. I came to understand that God was with me and comforted me as I mourned my mother.

Marlene's spiritual biography was quite different. Marlene told Reid that she and I were "both believers" when we married but noted, "I wasn't as strong a believer as him." Marlene fully embraced a personal faith in Christ when we had a growing family on Millar Road in Fraser.

At one point, she experienced back pain that kept her bedridden for several days. First, my father came and visited with her and read the Bible to her. Soon, Pastor Crain also shared the Gospel with her, and that's when she came to a personal relationship with Jesus Christ.

Together, our love for God only grew from there. Early in our marriage, we held Bible studies on the pool deck at Millar Road. We opened our home for Lakeshore's Vacation Bible School program each summer. I was on Lakeshore's board of elders. And when we began to attend Knox Presbyterian in the 1970s, our devotion to supporting our church became even deeper.

"We heard there was going to be a new church built at 16-Mile Road, and it was getting hard, with the distance, to keep the kids active at Lakeshore," Marlene recalled. "So we decided to change churches. Knox began meeting in a school. But then they built a church, and John helped. It became our bedrock."

Our friendship with Stewart Fleming, at Knox Presbyterian, and his wife, Francis, ended up being a crucial relationship for us and for our spiritual growth. The Flemings were Grace Fenton's parents. Chris Fenton, their son-in-law, was an elder of the church though still only in his twenties.

"John and Marlene loved my dad's Sunday School class and his teaching," Grace remembered. "John highly valued my dad. John had enormous strengths; so did my dad, in different ways, and they were a complement to each other."

Each of us had engineering backgrounds, for instance, with Stewart's stemming from his college degree—and mine from decades of experience in building things.

I leaned on Stewart a lot in the early days of my Christian walk. For instance, Grace recalled that I wasn't an eloquent public speaker, and so I'd ask her dad to write a prayer for me if I had to pray publicly. Her father was a tremendous sounding board for me when it came to theology and doctrine. If I had questions that couldn't be easily answered, Stewart took the time to research the topic and explain it to me. Those were the kind of things he loved to dwell on, according to his daughter, so we formed a great partnership.

Over the years, Knox Presbyterian Church became our second home and family. Our foundation has made several contributions to help ensure that Knox has everything it needs, including a new childcare wing, information desk for greeting visitors, and carpeting and paint in the sanctuary. In 2003, our foundation covered half the construction costs of a new $2.2 million activities center, which includes a full-scale gymnasium, a reception hall, a commercial kitchen, and classrooms.

Perhaps our most precious gift to the church, or at least the one that Grace enjoys the most, is a nine-foot, six-inch-long Mason & Hamlin grand piano, one of the largest musical instruments ever situated in the state of Michigan. The foundation donated it to Knox during the 1980s, and Fenton is fortunate enough to have been among its players for decades. We also were diligent to ensure the piano was properly maintained and even restored over the years.

⟨⟨⟨⟩⟩⟩

At some point, Marlene and I realized our faith in God would be the most important legacy we might leave. While I had grown fond of saying, "Trust me," to hesitant friends and relatives over the years, we ultimately responded to the highest calling: a God who said, "Trust me."

Over the coming decades, we wove our faith throughout our lives. Marlene, for instance, taught Bible Study Fellowship to women in the Grosse Pointes for eleven years. We also openly talked about God and faith to our children, grandchildren, and, well, anyone else who was willing to listen.

"Our prayer life as a family wasn't about praying that this mobile-home thing works out," Kristine said. "It was much deeper. And for us and their friends, watching their lifestyle was about watching how God would want someone to walk with Him. They're not perfect; they fail. But I'm always running into someone who says, 'Your mom just sat down and prayed with me.' "

From an early age, our grandchildren learned about God and Jesus Christ. When they were just tykes, Marlene urged them as soon as they were able to grapple with John 3:16: "God so loved the world . . . ." It is Marlene's favorite verse, so "she always wanted us to memorize that," Amanda remembered. Amid the coziness of our house in Beaver Creek, Marlene worked a lot with our grandchildren on memorizing Bible verses.

Our grandchildren also learned from "Nana" to generally trust in the Lord in every situation. Also, something as basic as praying before dinner was important. We paid for each of our grandchildren's annual stays at SpringHill, a Christian summer camp in northern Michigan, which we helped build. Abigail recalled, "We were given the opportunity to surround ourselves with other people of faith." Our grandson JT accepted the Lord as his Savior at a campfire during one summer camp.

Our faith meant everything to us, and we weren't bashful letting our children and grandchildren know it—even today.

As Anton, the namesake of his great-grandfather, said, "They keep bringing it to our attention that, with God, anything is possible. And they've shed a lot of light on that for us. They always practice their faith as well as share it with others."

"Though they put in the hard work, they acknowledge that it was trust and faith in God that made them what they are today," Abigail noted. "And as much as they valued education, they valued faith and our relationships with God so much more. We can all share that as common ground as a family, and a lot of families don't have that."

Added Alexandra, "Without the Lord, they know none of it was possible, and they credit him for everything."

Just as in the rest of our lives, when it comes to ministry endeavors, our motto has been, "Go big or go home."

One of my biggest long-term spiritual initiatives was helping get the Christian Business Men's Committee off the ground in Greater Detroit and playing a major role in sustaining it for decades. CBMC is an international evangelical Christian organization that began in Chicago in 1930, joined with similar groups to form a national organization in 1937, and moved its headquarters to Chattanooga, Tennessee, in 1978. Today it's known as the Christian Business Men's Connection and claims more than 50,000 members worldwide and a U.S. network of about 700 teams.

CBMC strives to encourage individuals to get connected and stay connected to help them grow in their faith. The group believes that "being strong in faith empowers men to share with others the good news of Jesus Christ in the marketplace and to live godly lives. By fulfilling God's purpose in their lives, men become a light to those around them by operating at a higher level of moral character and integrity and thus change the world around them."

In Metro Detroit in the early 1990s, CBMC had local staff but not yet a grassroots group of businessmen. When I caught wind of the need and the opportunity to spread the gospel, I leapt in headfirst. I was more than happy to be a foot soldier for Christ as well as a field general. Along with many others, I used my influence to help gather several hundred people annually for CBMC's big prayer breakfast at Cobo Hall in Detroit, or some other major venue, which regularly featured the mayor of Motown and other big hitters.

At the same time, I oversaw CBMC's boots-on-the-ground evangelization efforts, which involved an annual breakfast meeting and dispatching members, two-by-two, to visit their peers and witness for Christ. I was right out there among them, using my God-given talents and sense of humor to help the Holy Spirit open some doors, and some wallets.

Among other things, I also leveraged my position at the Grosse Pointe Yacht Club to benefit CBMC, exposing fellow boaters to the group and vice versa. GPYC became the home for the group for many big events—such as annual Christmastide banquets, where U.S. Senator Bill Armstrong and Prison Fellowship founder Chuck Colson were among the speakers— as well as weekly early-morning meetings.

Marlene also came into play regularly. She hosted CBMC gatherings at our home. And she ensured creative flair and quality control for the group's banquets—right down to making sure the decorations were GPYC quality.

Sharing the good news of the gospel isn't simply a suggestion. It isn't optional for Christians. It's a command that Jesus set for us—to share God's Word with others. "Go, therefore, and make disciples of all nations, baptizing them in the name of the Father and of the Son and of the Holy Spirit, teaching them to observe everything I have commanded of you," we are told in Matthew 28:19–20 (CSB). "And remember I am with you always, to the end of the age."

With grace and humility, Marlene and I have always sought to give back to the communities where we have lived, whether it was by supporting education, the arts, or health services. We have an overwhelming sense of gratitude to God for His provisions. More than anything else, we have an understanding that our greatest legacy will be having an impact on our world by helping others address moral and spiritual challenges, especially young people.

Jesus Christ is the anchor of our family, and so we hope to reach out to others around the world through various Christian ministries that can bring His life-changing love and message to them. That's why we have been so involved in ministries such as SpringHill Camps, YoungLife, Jesus Alive Ministries, Detroit

Rescue Mission Ministries, Joint Aid Management Ministries International in South Africa, and others. For children and young people, we hope to provide Christian guidance for a brighter future—and a much better world.

We have learned to understand that we are conduits to share the story of God's grace and mercy, and the world needs to hear it now more than ever. I know Marlene and I wouldn't be where we are today without our love for God, and that's the most important message we can leave behind.

CHAPTER 19
Roll Call of Gratitude

MORE THAN ANYTHING ELSE, AS CHRISTIANS, Marlene and I have always tried to live with compassion, empathy, and the will to make life better for others. As our companies became successful, we had a clear understanding that everything belongs to God, and it is our duty to give generously to those in need and to give cheerfully and with gratitude and sincerity, whether it was with our time, financial resources, or service.

In the 1980s, we established the John A. and Marlene L. Boll Foundation to share the resources that God has entrusted us with to various nonprofit charitable organizations around the world, including many in our home state of Michigan and other places where we became a part of the community. Since its inception, the foundation has pledged more than $55 million to Christ-centered organizations and other groups that share similar interests with us.

Our first priorities are Christian organizations, including churches, educational organizations, and missionaries. And, informed by Marlene's background, we like to help cultural and educational organizations. Community outfits such as law enforcement and hospitals comprise a third major focus for giving by the Boll Foundation.

Perhaps most importantly, almost every one of our gifts bears a personal stamp of interest that reflects how seriously we take our philanthropic mission. Our daughter, Kristine, is the executive director and, together with our board, we carefully follow our mission. We select recipients with intense care and prayer, and we follow up to make sure the charities are doing the wonders they promised when they received our gifts.

For example, our foundation gave an initial gift of $1 million to Prison Fellowship for a building the organization added on its campus near Washington, D.C., and named for Mike Timmis, our close friend who now is chairman of the fellowship board. Determined to continue supporting the unique mission of the organization, we have continued our giving to Prison Fellowship even in the wake of the passing of our dear friend, Chuck Colson, its bold and formidable founder, in 2012.

Three other important aspects of our philanthropy are continuity, accountability, and community. We typically don't just donate to a cause to see something built or a program launched, we also provide support to help ensure that a worthwhile initiative has the wherewithal to go on. We check in with the organization to make sure the money is being spent as promised and to find out what kind of refinements might have to be made. And, importantly, we encourage others to give along with us to see for themselves how their help can make a difference in the world.

Our attitude for giving stems from the parable of the widow's offering that Jesus told in the chapters of Mark and Luke in the Bible. It's the tale of a widow who gives only two small copper coins to the temple treasury. Jesus describes how great her gift is because it represents a much greater proportion of her resources than those given by religious leaders. It's a lesson we've tried to instill in our children and grandchildren—and one that we still follow today.

"Again and again, my father encourages me to say to our recipients that they should treat all their donors the same way," Kristine said. "Because remember, the 'little fish' who give $25 or $50 could become 'big fish' later. And it's just the right thing to do to treat everyone equally. They deserve respect."

Whether it's a large or small gift, we realize the importance of following through to complete what we've started. For instance, some years ago we accompanied Timmis on a mission trip to Africa and encountered an orphanage that needed a tractor to acquire feed for its cows, which in turn were crucial for supplying the kids with milk. We supplied them with a tractor.

"A few years later, the tractor needed repairs, and Mom and Dad stepped in," Kristine said. "They'd kept the tractor running for eight to ten years for that orphanage, but they weren't going to give up on it now."

Bob Henley, our good friend and pastor in Ocean Reef, described what he called the "Boll brand" in philanthropy as representing "integrity to the core and also things consistent with the tenets of the Christian faith."

"When they stamp their name on something, they know what that represents," Bob said. "Everyone knows what it represents."

From mentors such as Sam Frankel and others, I learned something from each man in terms of a mode of giving. One of them was that you could give it away in different ways than just writing a check, and to be good stewards, you need to go out and see what it is you're going to support. We still follow those principles today.

⸻

Of course, Marlene and I worked hard to be involved in the community long before we established a family foundation. Our philanthropy started with the gift of $2,000 to St. John's hospital in Detroit in the 1960s and grew from there.

SpringHill Camps in Michigan is one of the first organizations we decided to help and is a great example of our hands-on involvement. In 1967, the summer Bible camp of the Michigan Evangelical Free churches was failing. But Enoch Olson and another pastor fought for the denomination to expand this ministry rather than fold it, and they sought help for purchasing a rolling, wooded, 515-acre property outside Evart, a little town in the northwestern quadrant of the state.

They found their way to me and a few other Christian entrepreneurs, who banded together to buy the property and begin to build the camp. These successful businesspeople believed their kids would benefit and, perhaps, so would generations of children after them.

For me, helping launch a new Bible camp was like putting a kid in a candy store—or, rather, on a playground. While I was tremendously busy growing Chateau at the time, Marlene and I were determined to make SpringHill one of the best Bible summer camps in the country. Besides overall financial and moral support, I also helped fund what was like a giant Tinkertoy project. For example, I helped fund an idle train caboose and the fuselage of an old military airplane into early barracks for campers; both remain in use today.

As our children and, eventually, grandchildren, enjoyed SpringHill each summer, our support of the camp kept taking on new dimensions. Our commitment to SpringHill was tested in an unusual and unfortunate way in the late 1990s when Mark Olson, Enoch's son and head of the organization, fell seriously ill with leukemia. Mark was 40 years old, with a wife and four young children, and his family and the SpringHill community were understandably devastated when he failed quickly and died in 2001.

Marlene and I led an effort by SpringHill supporters to form a scholarship trust large enough to put all four kids through college, and our foundation made the initial contribution. I'm happy to report that all four children went through college without any debt.

We honored Mark in another way by bolstering SpringHill in the wake of his death. Our foundation donated $1 million as the lead gift for a multimillion-dollar new auditorium that seats up to 2,000 people for worship services, concerts, plays, and other activities that serve as the heartbeat of the collective SpringHill experience.

"The Olson Auditorium has allowed us to reach and serve more kids and amp up the quality of what we do," Michael Perry, who took over as president, said in a video. "When our quality goes up, the reputation of SpringHill goes up ... We've also allowed the community to use the auditorium; it's the only one within 30 miles. That has allowed us to reach and serve more kids."

And as with many other projects we have been involved over the years, we stuck around to help SpringHill actually build Olson Auditorium. Marlene, in particular, enjoyed lending her performing arts expertise to the project, similar to how she had influenced the architectural and design aspects of the Vilar Center in Beaver Creek.

"She was able to give us good feedback based on all of her experience," Perry said. "She focused on the stage and backstage. At one point we showed her plans for the green room, and she said, 'Where are the bathrooms?' We showed her our bathrooms off the lobby in the front of the building. But she said, 'When you're going to go on stage, you always have to use the bathroom, so you need to put it right here.' So we made the change."

Our foundation has continued to boost SpringHill over the years, including contributing the lead financial gift for upgrading a twenty-five-year-old indoor pool.

Now SpringHill has expanded with a camp in southern Indiana as well, and the two sites welcome about 50,000 campers each year, including many scholarship kids from low-income families.

As my business success and financial resources grew, Marlene and I were able to give to charitable groups in more systematic ways. Eventually we began to take on the excitement of becoming dedicated philanthropists. We came to realize that while gifts come in many shapes, sizes, and forms, the only true gifts are those that go on long after they are given.

Early on, we paid a lot of attention to institutions that were closely connected to our family, such as Knox Presbyterian Church, Christian Business Men's Connection, and the schools our grandchildren were attending. Countless times, we have lent Sugar Boll, our chalet in northern Michigan, to pastors, missionaries, and other Christian leaders in need of a beautiful place to rest, study, and relax. We donated half the money for the first van for my nephew Reid Nelson's church and then bought the entirety of a new one years later.

Another target of our charitable giving has been University Liggett School, the state's oldest independent coeducational day school in Grosse Pointe Woods. Six of our grandchildren went to school there. Our foundation made contributions over the years to expand athletic facilities, build a new media center, and create learning programs for kids with learning differences, including our grandson, JT, who is dyslexic.

Educational needs proved to be a major area where we broadened our giving beyond the sphere of our family's interests. A long-time administrator at Grosse Pointe Public Schools, Chris Fenton, was in charge of an $11-million addition to Grosse Pointe South High School for a gym, weight room, and pool, and the bond-issue project was coming up about $500,000 short. Our foundation ended up covering the shortfall.

Similarly, we have focused on other educational needs in Detroit, including helping a small group of reform-minded backers start Cornerstone Schools, a group of charter schools in the city that have gained a national reputation for excellence. They opened in 1991.

"We made a commitment with four other families to establish Cornerstone, including the Timmises and Van Elslanders, and at one point these five schools had about 3,500 children in them, mostly urban children," Marlene said. "As founders we had started them out as Christ-centered schools and accepted no money from federal or state government. So they could be taught Christian morals and values."

In 2015, Cornerstone graduated its first high school senior class of fourteen students. Each of the students was accepted to college and received scholarships totaling $1.5 million. One of young men went to Harvard University on a four-year scholarship.

Marlene's experience as a dancer guided her to focus on the performance arts when it came to philanthropy. Among the groups our foundation has supported includes the Detroit Symphony Orchestra, Michigan Opera Theater, Grosse Pointe Theatre, Vail International Dance Festival, and the Gerald R. Ford Amphitheater in Vail. One of my favorite projects was financing a Dutch room at the Detroit Institute of Art, which captured the art and culture of the seventeenth-century people of my parents' homeland.

When David DiChiera, head of the Michigan Opera Theater, enlisted our help to carry out his ambition of restoring an old building downtown to house his troupe, I led a few potential donors through where he wanted to move. We climbed up on the scaffolding and when we reached the top, we could see right through to the sky. Parts of the roof had decayed. With the help of a long list of individual, corporate, and foundation donors, the Michigan Opera Theater's renovation created one of the nation's best opera houses.

Not only did our foundation help spearhead the Detroit Symphony Orchestra's restoration of Orchestra Hall as its new home, but I was on the board for nine years and director emeritus for several years, and Marlene has led voluntarily councils and gala planning. She also brought her special touch to the DSO's green room, just as at SpringHill. "She imagined the room, which is beautifully refined and warm and intimate and yet a public room," said Anne Parsons, the DSO's president and chief executive officer. In a wonderful tribute, the symphony honored us as "Heroes" in 2016.

Funding medical research, health programs, and facilities that serve our community are another important aspect of our foundation. We established the Boll Center for Human Development inside the Neighborhood Club in Grosse Pointe, which allows families to receive pediatric physical, occupational, speech, and language services all in one place. Because of the health problems that JT endured as a child, we funded a new pediatric surgical waiting room at Children's Hospital of Michigan in Detroit and made a $250,000 gift to the Peña Colorectal Center at Cincinnati Children's Hospital. Our foundation also supports the Michigan Parkinson Foundation, Michigan Cancer Foundation, The Medical Center at Ocean Reef, and Wigs 4 Kids, which helps young patients dealing with hair loss as a result of treatment for cancer and other diseases.

Because of our love for being on the water and outdoors, conservation has been another important cause for our foundation. We have contributed to the Detroit Riverfront Conservancy and made a gift to help create the $3-million Dossin Great Lakes Museum on Belle Isle in the Detroit River, a new exhibition that became a huge boost to restoration of the historic island's iconic role in the cultural and social life of the city.

"John was a visionary there, because we showed him this opportunity amid the darkest days for Detroit and Belle Isle, in 2009 or 2010," said Bob Bury, who was president of the Detroit Historical Museum for many years. "He had no connection to Belle Isle or particular affection for it. But being a guy who is fond of the water and boating, he recognized the hidden-jewel component of the museum and the great potential that was there."

As I said earlier, philanthropy doesn't end with simply writing a check. Sure, the charities need money to keep their doors open and do their amazing work, but there's so much more that goes into it. It's about taking an active role, rallying your friends and family, and using your contacts and influence in the business world to help.

For example, with a group of other members we helped streamline Ocean Reef community's philanthropic efforts.

In order to streamline the philanthropic efforts, the group agreed to stage one massive fundraiser a year, and that's what we do today. The Ocean Reef Community Foundation raises millions of dollars for a number of charities. And we make sure that at least half of the money we raise goes to nonprofit organizations outside Ocean Reef, where there are so many needs. In 2021, ORCF provided more than $1.6 million to those groups, many of which service the areas in which Ocean Reef employees live.

Perry, the head of SpringHill camps, has witnessed our networking efforts.

"They don't just give money and back away," he said. "And they don't just help you with the project. They connect you with other people in their circles. They make introductions, via phone calls or sometimes when we were with them. They would say, 'Have you called this person?' and, 'Go see this person.' They would bring my wife, Denise, and me with them into public situations where they were around people who were their peers and their friends. They'd introduce us and promote SpringHill and talk about it. They would just help compound our success with this generous approach."

Bury recalled how we helped bring other donors to what is now called the John and Marlene Boll Gallery at the Dossin Museum.

"He told me how he'd had lunch with a colleague at the Grosse Pointe Yacht Club and persuaded him to drive down to Belle Isle, where he told the guy, 'You know what I'd like you to do is what I did,' " Bury said. "About eighteen months later, this person made a gift of the same size as John and Marlene's. That was the way that John leveraged his business acumen and his relationships and his peer group, comprised of many people with means like himself, to help others."

CHAPTER 20

Lasting Legacy

OUR INTEREST IN THE YOUNG MEN'S CHRISTIAN Association as an organization had roots in our family's membership in a YMCA in Macomb County. This was the one to which we had lent our pool on Millar Road for swimming lessons. Then Marlene and I had helped integrate the area's separate Young Men's and Young Women's Christian Association facilities.

We met Reid Thebault, the then-president and chief executive officer of the YMCA of Metropolitan Detroit, during a fundraiser for Leader Dogs for the Blind at the home of Art Van Elslander, the affordable furniture mogul and fellow Dutchman who'd moved next door to us on Lake Shore Drive in Grosse Pointe Shores during the 1990s.

At the time, Thebault was in the middle of his own $35 million capital development program to build a new downtown Detroit facility. The YMCA had pocketed $5 million dollars after eminent domain and the wrecking ball claimed its downtown building that was built in 1909, helping clear the way for construction of Ford Field, which opened in 2002. The organization meanwhile operated a number of other YMCAs in Metro Detroit.

Reid also had in hand a challenge grant from the Kresge Foundation that depended on achieving a number of benchmarks, including securing a single donor of $1 million or more. The Kresge Foundation, with headquarters in Troy, Michigan, was founded by businessman S. S. Kresge in 1924. He created and owned two chains of department stores, one of which was renamed Kmart in 1977.

Up until that point, Reid and his staff had struggled to identify and secure a $1 million donor. So much so that the reality of a sparkling new magnet for the community in the form of a new YMCA in downtown Detroit remained a pipe dream.

"I had done a lot of research on big donations to YMCAs, and the largest I could find in history was $85,000," recalled Reid, who by that time had spent nearly three decades as an administrator for the organization in Houston, Oklahoma City, St. Louis, and Dayton, Ohio, before coming to Detroit in 1999.

"That was a big gap. I would meet with [Kresge Foundation head] John Marshall and update him, and I would try to get him to be more flexible. What if the donor gave only $200,000 or $250,000? But he wouldn't budge. He said it was really important to find someone who puts the YMCA in a different light when the discussion involves major gifts. So our staff and board kept brainstorming and working on it."

I had breakfast with Reid shortly before I retired from Chateau Properties. Reid went through the pitch he usually shared with potential donors about the importance of a downtown Y for Detroit, and the details of the challenge grant, and where the entire campaign stood. He didn't yet have any drawings of a potential new building or even a definite site picked out.

Then I cut him off; I didn't want to hear any more about it.

"Marlene and I have been talking, and we'd like to do something to help the city, and we think the new downtown Y would be perfect," I told him. "And we'd like to be that $1 million donor."

I'm pretty sure I caught him completely by surprise.

"John, do I understand that you'd like to do this?" he asked me. I reaffirmed our decision to him.

I'm sure, in Reid's mind, Marlene and I seemed unlikely donors, at least not lead ones. When we left the city to live in the northeastern suburbs in the mid-1950s, we played out our lives there. In fact, I kept moving farther and farther out from the urban core of Detroit to build my properties in Michigan and, eventually, in many other states. Marlene and I added homes in northern Michigan, Colorado and Florida, not a condo on the Detroit Riverfront. I never even thought about putting Chateau communities in Detroit, if only because they wouldn't have fit my company's business model.

For whatever reason, and I guess it was God tugging at my heart, my emotions were circling back to my hometown as I neared the end of my business career. Detroit was where my parents staked their life's fortunes not long after getting off that boat at Ellis Island. It was the place where I learned to be a son and a brother and a husband, and the industrial setting where I acquired the skills and learned trades from so many hard-working Detroiters.

More importantly, Marlene and I also recognized the economic, social, and cultural importance to the region and the entire state, even to the country, of revitalizing Detroit. At the time, the Motor City was still experiencing its slide into the depressing debacle that climaxed in 2008 with the onset of the Great Recession and that culminated in the U.S.-taxpayer bailouts of General Motors and Chrysler in 2009. The accompanying economic disaster left parts of the city in ruins and the municipal government on the steps of the bankruptcy court in the Detroit federal building in July 2013. We saw the terrible conditions on Jefferson Avenue all the way from 8-Mile Road into the city. The city was the pits. It had to get cleaned up.

Others questioned why we would make a financial commitment to a place where we didn't live or work.

"Some people thought he was crazy to do the YMCA," said Bob Bury, who was president of the Detroit Historical Museum for many years. "John doesn't come to mind as one of the usual philanthropic suspects from the automotive realm, or the Birmingham-Bloomfield Hills [Michigan] philanthropic community. He was under the radar in Detroit, more of a Mount Clemens-Macomb guy. That's who he is.

"He wasn't on the board of the Detroit chamber of commerce or the Detroit Economic Club, those very Detroit-focused thins. But he has done a lot of things to benefit Detroit, starting with the Y."

John Guest, our chaplain and close friend, knew what was in our hearts.

"You see them grappling with the state of the world, and that takes them to the kind of poverty and self-destructiveness that you've seen in Detroit," John said. "They don't miss that. That's why they got into the business of helping bring new life and renovation to the blighted parts of the city. They are very down to earth. They don't drive by it; they lean into it. They care about ordinary folks who are struggling."

While our gift created a promising new threshold and satisfied the challenge grant, opening the gates to several million more dollars for the facility, the YMCA had to continue its campaign to reach the $35 million goal. It dragged on for another year, then two. "Capital campaigns have a life cycle, where you have a lot of energy in the first two-thirds of the effort, then you kind of hit a wall," Reid explained. "We were about $3.8 million short of our goal."

Marlene and I prayed about what to do to help even more. Our son-in-law Jim Mestdagh had joined the YMCA board in the wake of the first gift, and he went to a meeting of the organization at its northern Oakland County facility bearing an envelope in his sport-coat pocket. He handed the note to Reid as the meeting started, and the chief put the envelope in his own pocket. While one of his staff people was making a presentation, Reid opened the note, expecting nothing in particular.

The note said that we would be happy to add an additional $4 million to our giving for the facility, and that if it was possible, we wondered if the new downtown YMCA could be named after the Boll family. It also said that, if this weren't possible, we would still like to make the additional contribution.

"That literally put us over the top," Reid said. "It took every ounce of self-control at the meeting not to stand up and shout it out."

Marlene and I continued to demonstrate great interest in the project as it went forward. Initially, we weren't happy with the city block that Detroit cleared and donated for the new Y, an irregularly shaped parcel that is bordered by John R, Farmer, and Broadway streets and Grand River Avenue. "It's such a funny piece of property," Marlene said. "We wondered how they could build a Y there."

But we became encouraged when, after initial missteps with a handful of local architects, the YMCA enlisted a young whiz from Philadelphia who instinctively grasped the idea of "bringing the urban environment into the facility," as Reid put it.

From the extensive use of windows and open spaces to the fact that the new YMCA includes a stop for the city's People Mover, that's what was accomplished. How could you beat that? The People Mover goes by GM and other big buildings and then comes to the Y and unloads. So it's noon, and someone wants to work out for a half hour. They jump on the People Mover to the Y and back. Location became a real asset and is to this day.

Now, thriving start-up businesses, sleek hotels, and coffee shops surround the Boll Family YMCA in a revitalized urban neighborhood. Members and families are enjoying an indoor pool, rock-climbing wall, daycare center, the Marlene Boll Theatre, and continuing education classes ranging from photography to dance to computer tech. As Marlene put it, "The building kind of cleaned up that area. That's what a nice building does."

Matthew Piper, a writer and photographer who covers art, architecture, and sustainable development in Detroit, might have described the Y building best, when he wrote: "Extensive glazing throughout the building, meanwhile, transposes inside and outside to powerful, dramatic effect. From within, the ever-present window walls offer stunning views of the surrounding street life, richly crafted historic architecture, and glossy new developments, like the Z Lot, that echo the Y's crisp lines. From outside, the same windows engage passersby, inviting their attention and interest and enlivening the street."

The Y's commitment to downtown wasn't lost on Piper either. "The Boll Family Y says 'Yes' to the city. It opens its long arms to the urban fabric, and after decades of abandonment and near-fortification, this was not only an optimistic gesture, but a transformational one."

After the facility opened in 2005, some things had remained unfinished, including a planned half-million-dollar playground for the childcare center. The initial donor had backed out following the recession. We thought we might do something more to honor our grandson, JT, who had been through so much because of his health problems. We wanted to honor his courage and his effort and his love of his family.

When all was said and done at the new Boll Family YMCA, and the building staged a grand opening, all of our children, their spouses, and our grandchildren (who were mostly between the ages of seven and twelve at the time), were there to mark the occasion. I even found a way to extend an invitation to old friends. We invited the choir from Knox Church to come and sing from the balcony above where we were having lunch.

Finally putting our names on a philanthropic project—as we did for the first time with the Detroit YMCA and then with the gallery at the Dossin Great Lakes Museum—wasn't an easy decision. Previously, when we made major contributions to institutions and programs, we preferred to keep our roles low-key—and certainly not in lights. But when it came to the YMCA, we relented to all who advised us that lending our names could stretch the impact of the project. "They'd never named a building before, but they felt that if they did with the Y, others might follow and donate as well," our daughter Kristine said.

We still get to remain in the background. When we showed up unannounced at the front desk of the Boll Family YMCA on a Saturday with some friends who wanted to have a tour, we simply accepted a denial of the privilege because we weren't members. "They didn't say, 'But we're the Bolls,' " Kristine said.

If nothing else, I feel that our contribution has proved to be a valuable lesson to our grandchildren on the importance of philanthropy and helping others.

"It's wonderful to go downtown, walk around, and see their names on the YMCA building," said Amanda. "It makes you feel proud to know you have grandparents who have done so much for the community and who give their hard-earned money to people in needs like that."

CHAPTER 21

The Ties that Bind

OUR GRANDSON, JT MESTDAGH, WAS BORN IN
1995 with a life-threatening syndrome called VATER/
VACTERL, which brought with it a maddening array
of physical defects that added up to an essentially
non-functioning digestive system. His upper esophagus didn't connect to his lower esophagus and
stomach. JT had an imperforated anus. Moreover, the
baby's esophagus and trachea were conjoined, making
it very difficult for little JT to breathe at all.

And on and on—the bottom line was that the newborn JT couldn't consume or process any kind of nutrition, even water, and doctors had to operate immediately to save his life. Then every time the physicians discovered one condition and treated it, a new one would pop up. As a result, JT endured 250 days in hospitals before the age of three and sixteen major surgeries before he turned sixteen years old.

On top of that, as a third-grader, JT was diagnosed with dyslexia and severe short-term memory loss. By the time he was in fourth grade, his school told Kristine and Jim that JT would be illiterate for life.

As his grandparents, we pitched in with all our love, prayers, connections to the medical community, and financial resources to help their family deal with the unforgiving odds faced by little JT. We obtained the best and most informed care possible for our grandson. As he began to gain traction physically and grew, we also addressed JT's learning disabilities, helping send him to the highly regarded private University Liggett School in Grosse Pointe and even funding a new fast-reading program at several local schools. And, against all odds, JT did learn how to read.

"My grandparents have been right there with me every step of the way, whether it was on the medical or the educational side," JT said. "They were a big part of the journey."

John Guest, a family friend who pastored The Chapel in Ocean Reef for several years, called JT "a living example of what John and Marlene can help produce. JT acknowledges this—that all the medical care he's gotten, and the personal attention, and help in learning to read, and being able to do the things that he does, is because his family has gotten behind him.

"But I've never heard the family complain about what happened to JT, and I've prayed with them through all his struggles."

We tried to ensure our kids weren't spoiled even as our material success grew. This included requiring routine chores such as cleaning up the dinner dishes, even though Grandma Miller was available to do that for the many years she lived with our family. On Saturday mornings, the kids would wake up to a list of weekly chores we had compiled that included duties such as cleaning the boats, washing the car, mowing the lawn, planting flowers, vacuuming, dusting, and straightening up their rooms.

After we moved to the Lake Shore home and could afford contractors to do the work, the kids nevertheless had to pull all the old tile off the walls of several of the six bathrooms. Among other things, we wanted to communicate to our children the importance of a work ethic.

This discipline resulted in some incidents that the kids remember, largely in a humorous way, even today. During high school, for example, Kristine badly wanted an Izod shirt because "everyone in my class" at Grosse Pointe North had an alligator shirt," she said.

"But my dad said, 'A lot of kids would love an Izod shirt, and maybe you'll get one for your birthday. You don't need one right now,' " Kristine recalled. "I was accepting, and today I understand that, living through the Depression as they did, you don't forget certain things. He doesn't forget where he came from. There was always the thought in the back of his mind, 'Someday, I could be back where I started.' "

We also used axioms and other expressions of wisdom—as well as our everyday actions—to teach our kids lessons. When one would approach me about a challenge he or she was facing, I would say, "Problems are music to my ears, kid; have a seat." I also would share advice like, "Rise above the noise and keep your poise." Another classic, which I shared with my children when they felt intimidated or defeated, was, "They put their pants on the same way you do, kid."

Marlene would also weigh in with reminders such as, "The choices you make today will reflect the rest of your life." Our kids also learned as they aged the truth in another of Mom's favorite sayings, "Show me your friends, and I will tell you who you are."

But all of this advice was friendly rather than instructional, and I made sure a strong vein of humor ran through my family's home life. "I was out one night, and when I came home, Dad had filled my bed with M&Ms," Kristine said.

In 1976, our entire family visited Europe, uniting the kids with their relatives across the ocean—and bonding them more closely with one another. We took delivery of a flip-top camper in Wiesbaden, Germany, and it had a tent that you could extend out of the side. We spent six weeks there and met with all of my cousins and their children in the Netherlands. We also traveled in Austria and Switzerland and over to Italy. It was a great learning experience for the kids, and as a family, we grew a lot closer, because at home we were so busy all going in different directions.

John Jr. attended Albion College in Michigan and then graduated from Carthage College in Wisconsin, with an interest in business and, in particular, the construction arena where I had begun. He worked for a company in Atlanta for a couple of years and then, in 1985, joined me at Chateau. In 1993, John Jr. departed my company in the wake of the IPO. For the last several years, he has been in charge of the commercial division of Flame Furnace. "He does a great job," said Gary Marowske, Flame's owner.

John and his wife, Donna, have three daughters and a son: Amanda, Alexandra, Abigail, and Anton. Their family continues to grow with Nic, Alexandra's husband, and Andrei, who married Amanda in 2020 in our backyard at Lake Shore. They use the Sugar Boll house very often, following what John Jr. did as a child. John and Donna kept their kids active with sports and a lot of family time, similar to how he was raised.

Lora attended Grove City College in Pennsylvania, graduated from Hillsdale College, and then lived at our Grosse Pointe Shores home for a while, helping out where needed. She moved into her own house nearby and worked at local jobs for a few years before departing Michigan for Thunderbird School of Global Management in Arizona to earn her master's degree. Lora moved to California and had a job interview with Johnson & Johnson, where she met Sergio Mazza.

They married, and five months later moved to Lugano, Switzerland, and after six months relocated to Italy. Then they returned stateside, to Connecticut near Sergio's family, for about a decade. It was back to the Grosse Pointes for twelve years, then to Arizona in 2015. Along the way, Lora and Sergio had three children, Justin, Jaco, and Casey; and Sergio has a son, Alex, from a previous marriage. Justin and his wife, Margot, had their first child in 2021, and their daughter, Lilly, was our first great-grandchild. Their ever-growing family loved to travel and learn as they went, traveling especially around the United States and in Europe. More recently Lora and Sergio bought, and now are overhauling, a company in the Detroit area that provides management services for ambulatory surgical centers.

Kristine's path since her birth in 1965 as our first and only biological child very much has been that of an appreciative and dutiful daughter who has loved living in her parents' orbit and has correspondingly attended to many of our needs.

Jim Mestdagh met Kristine in high school, but they didn't date. While they were attending different colleges, he at Northwood University in mid-Michigan and she at Calvin College on the west side of the state, they formed a romantic attachment. Jim's courtship included creating a job cleaning boats at the Grosse Pointe Yacht Club on weekends, knowing that Kristine was on the docks as well, cleaning our family's boats.

I very much enjoyed spending time with Jim. I quickly learned that we're a lot alike when it comes to work ethic. One thing Jim liked is how I would insist on "doing the work" myself whenever possible, even long after I could afford to have it done by someone else. For instance, after Jim and Kristine were married, I wanted to put a Jacuzzi in our basement on Lake Shore.

"So here we were tearing out old hot-water tanks and busting out concrete basement floors ourselves," Jim recalled. "I'd help him on weekends. I remember saying to myself, 'He's a plumber by trade, but he's got 101 other things going on, and he can afford hiring someone else to put in a hot tub.'

"But no job was ever too big or above him, or below him. Even today, he would jump in first, from cleaning a table to tearing something else apart. People ask, 'Why would he do that?' He doesn't think that way—John believes that he can get the job done and doesn't need to pay some guy to do it. That was always impressive to me."

Early in their marriage, I tried to mentor Jim, telling him that if he ever wanted to get into real estate, he should learn both the banking and the building businesses. Jim first took a position as a bank-management trainee and then left to work for a general contractor in Detroit, learning both sides of the real estate coin as I had advised. After Chateau Properties went public in 1993, and John Jr. took over managing some of the residential and industrial developments that I still owned, Jim began to acquire more than twelve multifamily communities on his own. Today he manages my multifamily portfolio as well.

"He told me never to pass up an opportunity when a mentor invests in you," said Jim, who also helps Kristine run the family foundation. "And he invested more in me than anyone else has. John mentors anyone who will listen, and I was all ears."

We have doted on all of our grandchildren about as much as possible. JT noted that it's Marlene to whom the grandchildren most often turn for her thoughts on important matters. "She's the one who wants to sit down for a one-on-one," he said. "She's always, 'JT, come here for a minute and sit down and talk.' She wants to know how I'm doing. She's the one saying, 'How can I watch your podcast and tell my friends about it?' "

Meanwhile, I am more of the grandparent who provides them with "silent observation and wisdom, with storytelling too," said Alexandra. "He's a quiet character and mostly sits back and observes. He's a great listener. He's the quiet type, which means you never know what he's calculating. I wouldn't want to be a person who has to get into any ring against him."

Of course, I brought the same sense of humor to my relationships with my grandchildren as I had to other family members. I often subjected JT and Anton to fake spiders, snakes, and other creatures in their beds—even real-looking, but artificial, dog poop. I would put on a werewolf mask and pop out unexpectedly at Alexandra and the other kids in the basement at Grosse Pointe Shores. When visiting there, the grandchildren were continually exposed to an endless supply of "Silly String, Whoopee cushions, gag gifts, and those ridiculously large punch balloons," Abigail said.

Added Alexandra: "He will shove your face in a cake or get you candles that will relight when you blow them out, and you look like a fool. We were terrorized—and I say that in the best way possible."

———

JT has been able to channel the astonishing agony and incredible victories of his childhood experiences for the greater good. He has become an evangelist of sorts, fashioning a career at this point out of hosting a podcast and writing books—his first one, *Untether: Inspiration For Living Free and Strong No Matter What the Challenge*, was an Amazon bestseller—and making personal appearances as a Christian inspirational speaker.

That track record reminds many of me. JT agreed that he has a fiery attitude similar to mine: There's no giving up in his mind in any way. You push through. His personality is to keep going and get engaged. That's what has kept him so healthy.

Not surprisingly, we are very close. "Papi" is the one who dubbed him "JT" after Jim and Kristine named their baby James Thomas. "No one has called me anything else since," JT wrote in *Untether*. Years later, displaying a unique understanding of his struggle with dyslexia, I described JT's life as feeling "like he's living in a foreign country," and JT has used that illustration hundreds of times since.

The education of our grandchildren has been one of our deep and abiding interests. Our approach has been to facilitate life-long learning. For example, every Christmas, we took the grandchildren to the Rockettes show in Detroit or some other holiday event.

"We would learn from boat captains and pilots as we traveled," said Abigail. "On vacations with Nana and Papa, we would visit museums and parks and attend classical concerts. They never fail to pair learning opportunities with their grandchildren's interests," which for Abigail includes a passion for dance—like her grandmother's.

When Justin decided to make a career change and become a pilot, I provided the opportunity for him to fly with our pilots around the country on our planes. I wanted Justin to have a true taste of piloting in a sort of crash course so he could decide if it was really where he wanted to go with his life. For her 16th birthday, we took Amanda to New York City for a weekend, her first time there. On occasion, we would individually whisk off one of the grandchildren to Beaver Creek or Ocean Reef. And on and on.

One of my biggest ways to leave a stamp on my family was through a "scholarship" program that Marlene and I established to provide college financing for all participating grandchildren. Participating was a key word, because there were huge aspects of performance and accountability to the agreement.

Basically, we offered what amounted to contracts to each of our grandchildren: If he or she attended any school on a list of Christian or conservative-oriented liberal arts colleges and universities in Michigan for at least two years, maintained grades that reflected effort at a level at least equal to their capability and potential, and reported regularly on their progress to us, most of the costs of their education would be taken care of.

We felt it was important for our grandchildren to have "skin in the game" such as paying for their books, extra fees, and pocket money. In other words, we would continue through attainment of a bachelor's degree to pay for our grandchildren's schooling as we had shouldered much of the cost of their kindergarten-through-high school years. After that, if they wanted to pursue a master's degree or doctoral degree, they or their parents would have to pay for it.

"It strengthened our faith and got a lot of us to where we are today," said Amanda, who graduated from Hope College.

"How nice it is even now not to have to worry about student loans," Justin added. "They didn't have the opportunity to go to college. That's one reason they see the value in a college education."

It just seemed to make sense that if the kids were paying for part of their education and knew ahead of time that they had to live up to their goals and abilities, they would perform well—and they did.

CHAPTER 22

Only in America

IF YOU'RE FACING A HEALTH CRISIS, DR. TECH Soo is the kind of doctor you want not only in your corner but absolutely trusted with the results of your care. He's one of North America's most renowned neurosurgeons, with a Detroit-based practice group with about 28,000 patients a year and a record as a technology innovator in his specialty, including designing and contracting manufacture of surgical devices that have significantly advanced the treatment of back pain.

As much as I curried the trust of others, in later years I faced a couple of grave medical crises in which my faith in Dr. Soo—and in God—created monumental "trust me" moments for me.

In my earlier years, I had sustained a broken bone or two on the ski slopes and suffered other occasional accidents. My nephew, Reid Nelson, recalled the time we were chopping wood at his house. "He split his foot open with an axe," Reid said. "It scared the daylights out of me. Aunt Marlene and I were pretty excited as we saw the blood dripping. He didn't go to the doctor but put a special butterfly Band-Aid on it; it was a little bloody but not enough for a stitch, in his opinion."

Decades ago, I had both knees replaced. And for the last several years, I have tolerated pulmonary hypertension, which has limited my travels and ability to exercise. Most disappointingly, since 2019 I no longer can ascend to the high altitude of my home in beloved Beaver Creek.

As with many older people, our physical decline has been frustrating at times, but Marlene and I have done all we can within reason to keep it at bay. "They've been very attentive to their health over the years," said Steve Minnick, a family physician and friend. "For many years, they routinely went to Pritikin [Longevity Centers]. They did their best to stay in shape. They were very attentive to checkups.

"I would characterize their thinking as, 'If the good Lord is going to give us long and productive lives, we don't want to do things as individuals to upset that,' " Minnick continued. "John always had a sense that God was watching over him and that what would be, would be—medicine was just a handmaiden."

But my long and productive life was interrupted in 2009 by the first of two life-threatening moments. The first was related to my back. As Soo explained it, my height wasn't an advantage in my old age that it arguably had been for most of my life. "He is a man of tall stature who has extremely tall [spinal] discs," explained Soo. "So John tends to have more movement in his spine than normal. That subjected him to reduced abilities and degeneration."

For some time, Soo treated my back pain with epidural steroids and other noninvasive measures. I lived with it and conducted my normal high-activity life. But soon the pain and debilitation were just too great for me to bear, so I asked Soo to perform surgery on me. Soo did a "massive but minimally invasive" operation on me, reconstructing much of my spine and relying on his patented surgical devices. There were complications caused in part by how the hospital medicated me: I reacted allergically to a painkiller, causing me to retain an astounding 20 pounds of fluid. My heart also began to fail me. It was a very scary time.

"Spine surgery always involves a lot of bloodletting," Soo explained. "So John developed some dysfunction in the left part of his heart. He was in the cardiac ICU getting confused, huffing and puffing, and people holding a big needle wanting to tap the fluid. He was going down. His vascular system was leaky with no ability to pull back fluid from the soft tissue. John was going down."

So Soo made an "executive decision" and, without authorization and over the objections of the heart-intensive-care staff, wheeled me away to the neurosurgery ICU so he could direct my care. "We gave John a ton of diuretics and pumped him up with tons of Albumin," Soo said. "It was not a kosher way to do it and probably was risking my reputation, but he was going downhill. He was spiraling into an abyss. It turned out to be a stitch in time that saved nine."

In the end, Kristine observed, that I "went into Tech's office in a wheelchair, but after surgery he was walking."

A couple of years later, when I again needed a medical champion I could trust unhesitatingly, there was no doubt it was going to be Soo. On October 11, 2013, I was at home on a beautiful fall day with Marlene and our beloved Labrador, Duke. I was troubled by a headache and took an afternoon nap, which was unusual. Duke began paying extremely close attention to me, as if the Lab could detect that something wasn't quite right.

By evening, my distress had worsened into what I called a "monster headache," and Marlene said, "That's it. You never get headaches like this. I'm taking you to the ER." Marlene drove me to St. John's Hospital a few miles away, soon to be joined by Kristine and Jim. The staff diagnosed me with a cranial brain bleed and said I'd need emergency surgery.

It was about 11 p.m. on a Saturday, but Kristine called Soo anyway. At home, he quickly obtained a glance at computer records of my case. Soo immediately jumped in his car and raced from Farmington, about forty-five minutes from St. John's Hospital in Detroit, to try to save my life. While Soo wasn't a practicing physician at that hospital, but rather at St. John's Providence in Southfield, another suburb, nevertheless he called the ER treating me and said he would perform brain surgery on me. He asked to assemble a team to help him. Soo knew he would suffer a professional wrist-slapping—or worse—as a result. But that didn't stop him.

"In that kind of situation, there's just one focus, one objective: Time equals life," Soo explained. "Every minute means one more nerve cell could die. Every minute passed means three more months of recovery. All I knew was I had to stop the bleeding. It was almost like being naked without a weapon in the face of a lion. The staff didn't understand my accent, for instance. I told myself it was going to be fine, that I'd be able to slay the lion."

Indeed, as Kristine marveled, Soo "never had done surgery with this team" that was quickly assembled at the hospital during his drive there. "But he told us, 'You do what you need to do,' meaning pray, 'and I'll do what I need to do.' " Soo's team stopped the bleeding, but the next day it resumed, and they had to operate on me again. It wasn't clear how much longer the surgeries could backstop my deteriorating condition.

As Soo put it, "Everything is tenuous when you're approaching eighty-five years old. The machinery is worn out.

He was bleeding in the brain and dying. He was on two blood thinners, because the staff there had overmedicated him against the risk of stroke. He never stopped bleeding, and by the second surgery, he was dying again."

The second time, Soo, desperate for a new approach that would give me a decisive victory, turned to a serum from Germany that hadn't been used before to stop bleeding. It worked; and to this day, Soo keeps the serum in his back pocket only for similar grave cases. Only much later did I ask Soo if he really thought I would survive, and Soo said, far from reassuringly, "If you go out on a football field, do you ever think you're going to lose?"

By the third day, it was becoming clearer that the combination of prayer and Soo's intervention had saved my life at least twice. Still, it was a given that I was going to have severe brain damage because of how much blood had built within my skull, and for how long. Now the recovery process would begin, and there was simply no telling how complete it would be nor how long it would take.

Soo visited me faithfully every day for seven weeks. Marlene was resolute and prayerful. "She was steady as a rock," remembered Betty Bosch, who works at the Boll family offices. "She never said, 'This is horrible.' She was always levelheaded, saying, 'This is what we've got to do.' "

Soo said that he'd seen "a good brain during surgery" and felt that I eventually would regain most of my faculties. Soo also was encouraged because he knew I had a strong will—and a strong prayer life. But my doctor couldn't predict the course of my recovery.

Friends including Gabe Anton "would visit and leave in tears," Kristine said, "not knowing if he would live. Gabe was shaken up because he felt like my dad was 'supposed to be able to walk on water.' " Grace Fenton was in the room with me one time when I experienced about fifteen minutes of strokelike symptoms, and she feared it was the end for me.

JT would bring in Duke, my companion for a decade, and my grandson and the Lab would just sit by my bedside. I was continuing to struggle to make sense of my world and what had happened to me. "He was always asking me how that bridge was coming along that we were building and looking out the window to see it—that was the state of mind he was in," JT said. Everyone told me what happened, but I didn't remember a thing.

But soon, Grace was writing the words to familiar hymns on sheets of paper in big letters and taping them to a wall of my hospital room so that when I opened my eyes, I could see those words that I knew so well. And I did. I opened my eyes one day and began singing "Amazing Grace," and everyone sort of knew I was coming back.

As the swelling of my brain went down and the continual prompting of my loved ones began breaking through, I was beginning to make connections. My recovery continued to the point where after a few weeks, some strange scenes ensued in the hall. I had been on the St. John's hospital board for sixteen years, so I knew many of the doctors I encountered on my walks outside my room. Many of them told me, "You're not supposed to be here."

And, sure enough, just in time for Christmas, I pretty much recovered all my mental faculties. As Soo said, "He became quite witty again for someone who'd had two brain surgeries."

Marlene and I thanked God—and Soo—for sparing my life.

———

Marlene faced her own share of personal "trust me" moments when her quick wits, charm, and even dancer's agility were tested to the maximum, creating tests that drew on her faith in herself, in her husband, and in God.

One of them occurred in September 2019. Marlene was already recovering from a pesky injury to her right foot that she sustained on a flight of stairs, something even a lifetime of dance instincts couldn't help her avoid. Then on a routine errand to a tailor in St. Clair Shores, she experienced one of the biggest shocks of her life: a carjacking.

As she parked her car at a strip mall in front of the tailor shop and opened the door a few inches, Marlene was touched by the tip of a gun on her head. It made her turn, and she confronted a man who stood there and said, "Get out of your car." She complied. "Give me your rings," the robber said to Marlene as he got into her seat. He began to pull rings off her fingers, and she complained that he was hurting her.

"Let me take my rings off and give them to you," Marlene said calmly. Next her assailant tried to start the car without understanding that having the key fob in his possession wasn't enough. "Put your foot on the brake and then push the start button" on the console, Marlene coached him. He started the car and took off, throwing Marlene's emptied wallet on the pavement in the process—and forgetting to demand the rings, including her wedding ring, that were still in her hand.

Obviously, Marlene was shaken. My response to the news was "poker straight," Kristine said, guessing that the incident brought back memories of my mother's murder. Police found the Bentley later that day, a few miles away and undamaged. But they weren't able to find the criminal.

What if Marlene hadn't had the composure, in that disorienting and terrifying moment, to respond calmly as she did? Someone that desperate to steal a vehicle, in broad daylight, might have been high or mentally unbalanced, and he was armed. Faced with the frustration of not being able to figure out how to get the car started and escape quickly, there's no telling how he might have taken it out on Marlene.

Within a few weeks, however, Marlene could talk about this jarring turn of events with her usual calmness, born of her conviction that God had protected her in that moment—a conclusion reflecting the fact that she and I willingly had lived our entire lives in the shadow of His grace and utterly depended on it.

⌒

As I look back at my ninety-two years on Earth, I often find myself reflecting on how my life has been affected by an ultimate "trust me" moment—not mine, but my father's. He walked away from his family and came to this country in 1923, not knowing the language or having a formal education. He left all that he ever knew and came here. My mom made those same difficult choices, too. Often I've wished they were still here so that I could ask them, "What made you do that?"

I was thinking about that mystery when I attended a charity fundraising dinner where Evan Bayh, a former U.S. senator and governor of Indiana, was the keynote speaker. I was seated next to Bayh during the dinner and began to share much of my own story with the renowned Democratic politician. Bayh asked me, "Where did you go to college?"

"I didn't," I told him.

"How did you get started?" he asked.

"All I had was a wheelbarrow and a shovel and went around looking for jobs," I replied.

A few minutes later, when it was time for Bayh to get up and speak, he suddenly referred to me, and says, "Only in America can this happen!"

He pounded his right fist into his left hand. Then he did that a couple more times.

"Only in America!" Bayh said. "Only in America can you start with a wheelbarrow and a hand shovel and thirty years later your company is listed on the New York Stock Exchange."

And maybe that's what my father saw too.

After years of thought and wonder, all I can conclude is that Anton Boll certainly was trusting in God's will and in His provision for his own life. But my father also trusted in his eventual offspring to manifest in what the Bible calls "the fullness of time"—the ultimate meaning of the transatlantic journey he took with my mother.

Now their great-grandchildren are beginning to understand how that legacy has taken shape through us.

"You don't see the kind of thing he created, starting with a shovel, being done now from scratch," Alexandra said. "It makes you appreciate what Nana and Papa did that much more. They saw that anything was possible, but they had to achieve it."

Only in America.

Endnotes

1. Brené Brown, *Dare to Lead* Training Program, September 2019, https://daretolead.brenebrown.com/.
2. Ellie Lisitsa, "The Four Horsemen: Criticism, Contempt, Defensiveness, and Stonewalling," The Gottman Institute, April 23, 2013, https://www.gottman.com/blog/the-four-horsemen-recognizing-criticism-contempt-defensiveness-and-stonewalling/.
3. The Albert Team, "Positive and Negative Feedback Loops in Biology," Albert (website), June 1, 2020, https://www.albert.io/blog/positive-negative-feedback-loops-biology/.
4. Geoff MacDonald and Mark Leary, "Why Does Social Exclusion Hurt? The Relationship Between Social and Physical Pain," *Psychological Bulletin* 131, no. 2 (April 2005): 202–223, https://www.researchgate.net/publication/7994338_Why_Does_Social_Exclusion_Hurt_The_Relationship_Between_Social_and_Physical_Pain#:~:text=MacDonald%20and%20Leary%20(2005)%20conducted,experienced%20as%20painful%20because%20%22reactions.
5. Mark Twain, *Adventures of Tom Sawyer* (The Heritage Press, 2000).
6. Emma Young in *New Scientist* magazine, October 9, 2018.
7. Richard Rudd, *Gene Keys: Embracing Your Higher Purpose* (Watkins, 2015).
8. Brené Brown, "Listening to Shame," TED Talk, March 16, 2012, https://www.ted.com/talks/brene_brown_listening_to_shame?language=en.
9. Brené Brown, "Shame vs. Guilt," Brené Brown (blog), January 14, 2013, https://brenebrown.com/blog/2013/01/14/shame-v-guilt/.

10. Stephen B. Karpman, *A Game Free Life* (Drama Triangle Publications, 2020).

11. Julia Cameron, Artist's Way (Jeremy P. Tarcher/Perigee, 1992)

12. NaniLea Diamond, Full Glory Live, accessed April 15, 2021, https://www.nanileadiamond.com/home.

13. "About Us," Somatic Experiencing Trauma International (website), accessed April 14, 2021, https://traumahealing.org/about-us/.

14. Diamond, Full Glory Live.

15. Lauren Landry, "Why Emotional Intelligence Is Important in Leadership," *Harvard Business Review*, April 3, 2019, https://online.hbs.edu/blog/post/emotional-intelligence-in-leadership.

16. Inspired by author's work with NaniLea Diamond.

17. Matt Kahn, *Whatever Arises, Love That: A Revolution that Begins with You* (audiobook), (Sounds True, 2016).

18. Rudd, *Gene Keys*.

19. Rudd, *Gene Keys*.

20. Kahn, *Whatever Arises*.

21. Catherine Price, "Putting Down Your Phone May Help You Live Longer," *New York Times*, April 24, 2019, https://www.nytimes.com/2019/04/24/well/mind/putting-down-your-phone-may-help-you-live-longer.html.

22. Price, "Putting Down Your Phone."

23. Shane Parrish, "Sheila Heen: Decoding Difficult Conversations," Knowledge Project Podcast, episode #57, accessed April 14, 2021, https://fs.blog/knowledge-project/.

24. Parrish, "Sheila Heen."

25. Antonio Demasio, *Descartes' Error: Emotion, Reason, and the Human Brain* (Penguin, 1994).

26. Albert Mehrabian, *Nonverbal Communication* (Routledge, 2007).

27. "Co-Active Is the New Language of Leadership," Co-Active Training Institute, accessed April 15, 2021, https://coactive.com/.

28. Kyle Cease, "Evolving Out Loud," Dolby Theatre performance.

29. Steve Jobs, "'You've Got to Find What You Love' Jobs Says" (Stanford Commencement Speech), Stanford News, June 14, 2005, https://news.stanford.edu/2005/06/14/jobs-061505/.

30. "Co-Active Is the New Language of Leadership."

31. Henry Ford, *My Life and Work* (Garden City Publishing, 1922).

32. "What Is the Placebo Effect?," WebMD, February 8, 2020, https://www.webmd.com/pain-management/what-is-the-placebo-effect.

33. Johann Hari, *Lost Connections: Uncovering the Real Causes of Depression—and the Unexpected Solutions* (Bloomsbury Publishing, 2019).

34. Rhonda Byrne, *The Secret* (Atria Books, 2006).

35. Benjamin Radford and Mary Carmichael, "Special Report: Secrets and Lies," *Skeptical Inquirer*, March 29, 2007.

36. Robert A. Scheinfeld, *Busting Loose from the Money Game: Mind-Blowing Strategies for Changing the Rules of a Game You Can't Win* (Wiley, 2006).

37. Dr. Joe Dispenza, *Becoming Supernatural: How Common People Are Doing the Uncommon* (Hay House Inc., 2019).

38. Philip B. Clarke et al., "The Straight Path to Healing: Using Motivational Interviewing to Address Spiritual Bypass," Journal of Counseling & Development 91, no. 1 (January 2013): 87-94, https://onlinelibrary.wiley.com/doi/abs/10.1002/j.1556-6676.2013.00075.x.

39. Charles B. Ferster and B. F. Skinner, *Schedules of Reinforcement* (Appleton-Century-Crofts, 1957).

40. Cease, "Evolving Out Loud."

41. Learned from author's work with NaniLea Diamond.

42. Homepage, Strozzi Institute, accessed April 15, 2021, https://strozziinstitute.com/.

43. Jobs, " 'You've Got to Find What You Love.'"

44. Meredith Hart, "The 100 Most Famous Quotes of All Time," Hubspot, accessed April 15, 2021, https://blog.hubspot.com/sales/famous-quotes.

45. Hart, "The 100 Most Famous Quotes."

46. Hart, "The 100 Most Famous Quotes."

47. Hart, "The 100 Most Famous Quotes."

48. Caroline Myss, *Energy Anatomy* (audiobook) (Sounds True, 2001).

49. Inspired by author's work with NaniLea Diamond.

50. Karpman, *A Game Free Life*.

51. Learned from, Rudd, *Gene Keys*.

52. Paraphrased, Rudd, *Gene Keys*.

53. Diamond, Full Glory Live.

54. Learned from, Cease, "Evolving Out Loud."

55. See Lisitsa, "The Four Horsemen."

56. Inspired by author's work with NaniLea Diamond.

57. Inspired by author's work with NaniLea Diamond.

58. Inspired by author's work with NaniLea Diamond.

59. Peter S. Beagle, *We Never Talk about My Brother* (Tachyon Publications, 2009).

60. Homepage, Eckhart Tolle (website), accessed April 15, 2021, https://eckharttolle.com/.